SILENT LANDSCAPE

BATTLEFIELDS OF THE WESTERN FRONT
—— ONE HUNDRED YEARS ON ——

WRITTEN BY SIMON DOUGHTY

PHOTOGRAPHY BY JAMES KERR

Helion & Company Limited
26 Willow Road
Solihull
West Midlands
B91 1UE
England
Tel. 0121 705 3393
Fax 0121 711 4075
Email: info@helion.co.uk
Website: www.helion.co.uk
Twitter: @helionbooks
Visit our blog http://blog.helion.co.uk/

Published by Helion & Company 2016
Book and cover design by James Kerr (www.silentlandscape.com)
Typeset by Mach 3 Solutions Ltd (www.mach3solutions.co.uk)
Cover composed by Paul Hewitt, Battlefield Design (www.battlefield-design.co.uk)
Printed by Gutenberg Press Limited, Tarxien, Malta

Text © Simon Doughty 2016
Images © James Kerr 2016
Map © Barbara Taylor 2016

ISBN 978-1-911096-03-0

British Library Cataloguing-in-Publication Data.
A catalogue record for this book is available from the British Library.

For details of other military history titles published by Helion & Company Limited contact the
above address, or visit our website: http://www.helion.co.uk.

We always welcome receiving book proposals from prospective authors.

FRONTISPIECE
Canadian Memorial at Vancouver Corner, Ypres.

"This villanous saltpetre should be digg'd
Out of the bowels of the harmless earth,
Which many a good tall fellow had destroy'd
So cowardly; and but for these vile guns,
He would himself have been a soldier."

William Shakespeare – Henry IV, Part I

CONTENTS

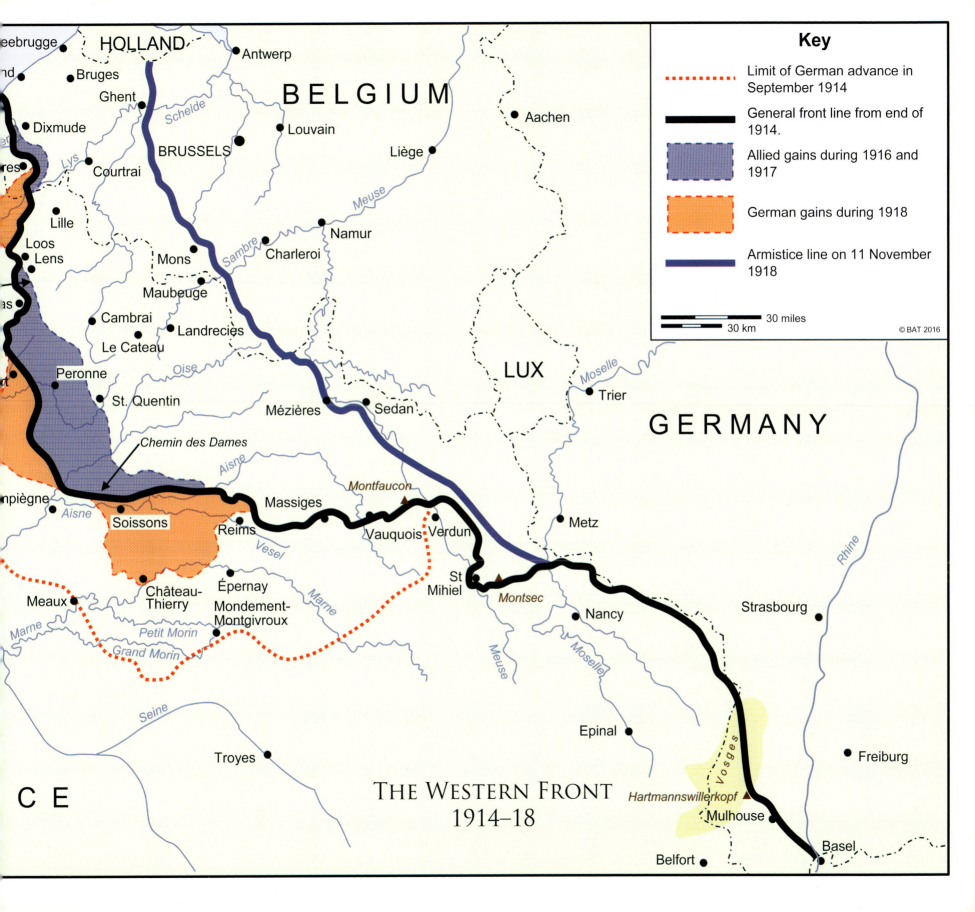

THE WESTERN FRONT
1914–18

Key

- Limit of German advance in September 1914
- General front line from end of 1914.
- Allied gains during 1916 and 1917
- German gains during 1918
- Armistice line on 11 November 1918

30 miles
30 km

© BAT 2016

HOLLAND

BELGIUM

GERMANY

LUX

FRANCE

Zeebrugge · Antwerp · Bruges · Ghent · Louvain · Aachen · Dixmude · Liège · Ypres · Courtrai · BRUSSELS · Lille · Namur · Loos · Charleroi · Lens · Mons · Maubeuge · Cambrai · Landrecies · Le Cateau · Peronne · St. Quentin · Méziéres · Sedan · Trier · Arras · Compiègne · Chemin des Dames · Soissons · Massiges · Montfaucon · Metz · Reims · Vauquois · Verdun · Meaux · Château-Thierry · Épernay · Mondement-Montgivroux · St Mihiel · Montsec · Nancy · Strasbourg · Troyes · Epinal · Freiburg · Hartmannswillerkopf · Mulhouse · Belfort · Basel

Schelde · Lys · Meuse · Sambre · Oise · Aisne · Vesel · Marne · Petit Morin · Grand Morin · Seine · Moselle · Moselle · Meuse · Rhine · Vosges

PREFACE

This book is the product of much talking, contemplating, and visiting the First World War battlefields of France and Flanders. Our idea was to focus on the landscape over which the war was fought – this narrow stretch of mostly rural countryside where the armies faced themselves for four years. Much has been published and written about the human dimension, the huge cost in lives, the impact on the political map of Europe, and all the other consequences of this shattering war; so we wanted to try a different emphasis. Because this was for the most part a static war fought with all the might of industrialised nations, it has left an indelible mark upon the landscape, an aspect that this book seeks to highlight.

We considered a before and after approach. There exists a rich photographic First World War archive, augmented by landscapes painted by war artists at the front, so it was tempting to present these alongside contemporary images. But we soon decided on something entirely modern: a photographic record of what these battlefields look like today, 100 years on.

Any book about the First World War must carry, first and foremost, a dedication to those who suffered: the servicemen and women who lost their lives or whose lives were blighted through injury; and, of course, the families who lost loved ones. But we would also like to dedicate this book to the many custodians of the landscape itself: the farmers and landowners who have brought their land back to life, the gardeners who have cared for the cemeteries and memorial parks that commemorate human loss, and the local people of later generations who have lived on or close by these battlefields.

In photographing and writing this book, it seemed to us that one of the most remarkable, and perhaps unique features of this war, is that so many of the topographical and physical features have remained. There are many scars and traces of war on the Western Front, along with the post-war cemeteries and memorials that are now integral to the landscape. All this will hopefully remain, in perpetuity, bearing witness to this and future generations.

Simon Doughty
James Kerr
May 2016

THE SOMME
Mesnil Ridge and Knightsbridge Cemeteries Mesnil-Martisart

INTRODUCTION

YPRES
Shell holes at Sanctuary Wood.

This book is about the landscape of the Western Front, where the First World War was fought relentlessly for over four years across a narrow 450 mile ribbon of Europe. It was here that the first big clashes took place following the German invasion in August 1914; it is where most of the decisive battles were fought; and it is here that the war ended in November 1918 with the final defeat of Germany. All the explosive and destructive power then known to man was used on the Western Front, with success and failure measured in yards rather than by human cost. The character of the landscape was soon lost once the battles started in earnest, stripped bare of vegetation and topsoil, churned beyond recognition, with irrigation systems destroyed, woods and forests erased, explosives littering the ground, and the remains of many thousands of soldiers lying on the battlefields.

In the 1920s and 30s the towns and many of the villages were rebuilt, removing the obvious physical traces of war except, of course, for the memorials and cemeteries created specifically for the purposes of remembrance. The bodies of 'the fallen' still on the battlefields were gradually gathered in and buried, although even today the ground can occasionally reveal the remains of a soldier killed a century ago.

It took years before farmers were safely able to return to their land, and there has always remained a risk of exploding ordnance. Fatalities among civilians were a regular occurrence but, all these years later, they can still happen when the ground gives up yet another live shell. In the rural areas intensive farming across the landscape has removed many of the traces of war, but physical scars do still remain and some are indelible. Deep craters have in places been filled with water, now providing a scene of tranquillity in stark contrast to the massive explosions that created them. Areas of woodland, mostly destroyed during the war, have grown back and now provide some protection for the landscape as it was then. Modern autoroutes traverse some of the battlefields while older roads and tracks, major thoroughfares during the war, have become quiet and overgrown.

There are places where imagination is needed to peel away today's urbanised landscape, but there are many other places where this is not necessary, particularly on a cold winter's day when the wind bites and the ground is hard with frost. Somehow, the landscape has absorbed the events that occurred here, even where the physical evidence is not immediately at hand. There is a presence, and there are places along the Western Front where this lingers extremely heavily.

Stand in a small copse in the centre of a field on the Somme, and that small patch of ground can reveal the pock-marked traces of war that the farmer's plough has gradually removed in the surrounding area. Even those open fields themselves can reveal the chalk-like shadows of the deeply dug trenches that once zig-zagged across the landscape. Take a look over the low garden-like wall of a cemetery where soldiers have been buried by their comrades in their own trench, and the sunken ground of that same trench can just be seen trailing into the undergrowth.

Some traces of the First World War have been intentionally preserved on the Western Front, and here one sees a landscape that has been softened by time, the ragged edges grassed over, the trenches lined neatly with concrete sandbags, trees planted where once had been wasteland, with paths laid across No Man's Land.

The extent to which the landscape of the First World War still carries evidence of conflict, so many years on, is a unique phenomenon. This was a war in which the fighting bore heavily on the ground, the physical places where this great clash of arms took place over a confined area. Modern weapons such as heavy artillery and machine-guns gave all the advantages to the defender, making the act of advancing and seizing ground all but impossible.

Once the infantry left the relative safety of their trenches and deep dug-outs and advanced into the open expanse of No Man's Land, they were vulnerable to the enemy's firepower, launched from their own trenches or from areas well beyond the line of sight of their opponent. The consequence of this was that rarely during the war could offensives be regarded as decisive, because they failed to break out from the confines of these small battlefields. Fighting was at close range, and territorial gains were often transitory, with ground changing hands in later fighting. The battlefields themselves, the front line trenches and the areas of broken landscape in between, were fought over time and time again.

For those who visit the battlefields, it is natural to start in nationally and culturally familiar surroundings. Somehow, the Somme 'feels' like England, similar to the downlands of Hampshire and Wiltshire, perhaps because there is so much evidence of the British presence here: the cemeteries, the names on gravestones and memorials, the place signs in English. But this reveals only a fragment of the story, and it is not until one ventures beyond these little English country gardens, these corners 'of a foreign field' that are '…forever England' that the perspective broadens to a more balanced picture of the vastness and terrible truth of this war. Soldiers from many nations, not just from Europe, were here. They fought perched on mountainsides, on flatlands from boggy water-filled trenches, in tunnels below ground, in stone-clad bunkers, in rainstorms, snowstorms, and on days when the sun shone relentlessly and when darkness only afforded a few hours of relative safety. And when it came to death and the ritual of burial and remembrance, the differences between national convention and styles vary dramatically. These places need to be seen to be in any way understood.

The Western Front continued to be pounded until finally, in 1918, mobility was restored to the battlefield. In time, the landscape, with all its restorative qualities, began a natural process of regeneration, with the physical traces of war melding into their surroundings. The other enduring legacy, the cemeteries, memorials, preserved trenches and battlefields, carefully tended as gardens and parkland, have given an ordered sense of humanity to these places. They are now part of the landscape as if they had always been there, as indeed they always will be, in perpetuity.

There are many victims of war, mostly human, but it might also be said that the landscape has suffered as well. It has been deeply scarred and damaged, and much of what existed there prior to the war was destroyed. The landscape was pressed into service by the opposing armies, and neither side worried about the damage they caused. They built deep trenches and dug-outs and tunnels below ground, laid railways from the rear areas to the front line, created supply depots and transit camps, requisitioned buildings for hospitals and headquarters, imported stone and aggregates to build roads. They attempted to impede the enemy by laying barbed wire some of which can still be found there today. Then, having built their own defences, they each sought to destroy their enemy's, by artillery bombardment, mines placed deep in the ground, bombs from aeroplanes above, by infantry assaults, later supported by tanks crawling across the countryside. Those physical scars along the Western Front have left an indelible reminder of how the landscape itself was affected. Like many victims of war, the landscape is innocent. The earth itself is harmless, it protects, is reliable and productive, it is the 'good earth'. It is man that uses the earth to his own ends. But thankfully the landscape can recover, as it has along the Western Front, with or without the help of man.

VERDUN
Remains of the Ouvrage de Thiaumont.

ENCOUNTER & RETREAT

CASTEAU MEMORIAL
Some three miles north of the Mons Canal is a memorial to the first encounter between British and German Cavalry.

OPENING BATTLES OF MOVEMENT

The early encounters of the war came as a great shock to the opponents and bore little resemblance to the trench warfare that followed, the battles that endure in the memories of later generations. It was only following those brief but violent engagements of August and September that the Western Front began to take shape, along the line to which the Germans retired following their failure to finish the war quickly, as they had hoped. Grand strategies often go awry, and in this case it was a combination of meddling with a sound plan, the frictions of war, and a determined opponent, that led to early German failure, stalemate, and a war for which no one was prepared nor wished to fight.

The Germans crossed the border into Luxembourg on 2nd August 1914, and were close to the Belgian city of Liège the following day. The British declaration of war came at 11pm on 4th August, and within two weeks the British Expeditionary Force had arrived in France, taking up their pre-determined positions near Maubeuge, 12 miles south of Mons and on the left of the Allied line.

In those early weeks, there was at least some vestige of familiarity with the wars of the past, and the cavalry were in their element. With little knowledge of German intentions and dispositions, small mounted detachments were out ahead of the infantry, searching for the enemy. The first contact was at about 06:30 on the morning of 21st August 1914, when a patrol of Prussian Uhlans was spotted by soldiers of the 4th Dragoon Guards close to the village of Casteau. The clash came as the Dragoons took the cold steel of their swords to the Uhlans and, within a few moments, a British officer killed a German by thrusting his sword into his chest, while a British corporal was the first to fire a rifle in anger. The officer's sword was of course something from the past, while the carbine, although not new in design, was similar in dimension and purpose to the rifles carried by cavalrymen of the 21st century.

The Battle of Mons, on 23rd August 1914, was the first of the war to be fought by the British Army. It was an 'encounter battle', the consequence of dispositions that had been agreed with the French prior to the outbreak of war. By a twist of fate, the British had been placed on the German axis of advance to Paris, making a clash of arms inevitable. Those early cavalry encounters and reconnaissance reports, along with sightings by the Royal Flying Corps, removed any doubt: the German First Army, under the command of Generaloberst von Kluck, was sweeping around Brussels, en route to Mons.

When the battle came, it lasted just one day, but that is to underestimate the ferocity and violence that unfolded, with the II (British) Corps commanded by General Sir Horace Smith-Dorrien outnumbered two-to-one and facing an entire German army. Most of the British infantry had only arrived the previous day, with barely time to dig rough entrenchments that were nothing like the deep and well-prepared trenches that came later. Some of the infantry on the Mons-Condé Canal built barriers across the roads and occupied nearby houses. But with no enemy in sight, there was still an air of deference about the local population and their property. The wholesale and systematic use of the landscape, both natural and man-made, only came later. At Mons, there was less inclination and, in the event, no time.

When the German artillery opened up on the British infantry at dawn on the day of battle, its scale and accuracy was unprecedented; a shock to the defenders and an early indicator that there was more to come in this industrialised war. But equally, the Germans were initially repelled by the rapid and heavy fire of the British riflemen. One German officer later claimed his soldiers 'were opposed only by machine-guns, but they were numerous, fired brilliantly, and were so well placed as to defy detection…' In reality, he had been facing British Infantrymen who relied upon disciplined rifle fire at 15 rounds per minute.

The Battle of Mons could never have been a British victory. The size of the German attack, and the weakness of the flanks, predicted that sooner or later retreat would be necessary. But neither was Mons a defeat. The heroism and steadfastness of this 'contemptible little army' was what carried the day, proving that it is often the early battles that have the true significance, long before any tide has changed.

The town of Mons recovered to an extent from the short battle, although life would never be quite the same for the local inhabitants. Many of them had been summoned by church bells on the morning of the battle and 'were seen in their best attire going to worship as if war was utterly distant from them'. Thankfully the physical damage and the human losses in and around the town were confined to just one day, but this was to be followed by the privations of a German occupation that lasted nearly to the end of the war, when there was again fighting in Mons, just before the Armistice on 11th November 1918.

Mons Canal at Nimy

The 4th Battalion The Royal Fusiliers held this section of
the Mons Canal, and it is here that Lieutenant Maurice
Dease and Private Sidney Godley won their Victoria Crosses,
defending a stone railway bridge with a machine-gun. The
original bridge was later replaced. Maurice Dease was killed
during the action, and is buried nearby at the St. Symphorien
Military Cemetery. Sidney Godley was wounded and then
captured by the Germans. He spent the remainder of the
war in a prisoner of war camp, and it was while in captivity
that he learnt of his Victoria Cross.

Retreat from Mons

Retreats can be ragged and sometimes shameless affairs, rarely remembered with much pride; the fact
that the British lost more casualties on the day following the Battle of Mons is perhaps indicative of
this. It is sometimes easier for history to record events that have some shape and form, while a military
retreat can be such an overwhelming and confusing experience that it defies easy explanation. The
Retreat from Mons was the longest in the British Army's history, and although not its finest moment,
it deserves to be remembered. For the soldiers, it was a gruelling experience. Long days on the march,
with little sleep and food, and generally no idea about what was happening or where they were going,
punctuated by local 'rearguard affairs' – clashes with the advancing German army.

Right:: Pave Road near Audrignies

Marching on the cobbled pavé was hard, particularly for the reservists who had re-joined their
regiments and were still 'breaking-in' their new boots. Sometimes marching on the hard stones in the
middle of the road seemed preferable to the dust in the gutter, and soldiers would change places when
the column halted briefly. The truth is that the novelty never lasted long, but at least the soldiers were
together, thinking not about the battle ahead but the next time they would sit down and sleep.

LE CATEAU

The Battle of Le Cateau was more than a 'rearguard affair', and proved to be both a vital and unavoidable action that did much to save the British Expeditionary Force (BEF) in August 1914. The commander of II Corps, Horace Smith-Dorrien, had been ordered to withdraw by Field Marshal Sir John French, Commander-in-Chief of the BEF, but reality had presented him with a stark choice. Either he risked being overcome by the Germans as he fought numerous costly engagements, or he turned to face the enemy to deliver a stopping blow from which he might be able to break clean and get away to fight another day. He chose the latter, ordering II Corps to set up defensive positions near the town of Le Cateau on the evening of 25th August. The following morning, the Germans attacked with nearly twice the combat strength and all the momentum of an advancing army. The British held steady and firm on a stark and open battlefield, devoid of cover and with only the most rudimentary defences. A combination of rapid rifle and artillery fire inflicted heavy losses on the enemy, temporarily bringing the German advance to a halt. But as with all delaying actions, this could do no more than buy time for escape. By the afternoon the British flanks were beginning to give way, and Smith-Dorrien ordered his corps to withdraw. Casualties on both sides were heavy, and although Sir John French initially praised his subordinate for the bold action that had 'saved the left wing' of the BEF, by the following year he had rather changed his tune, describing Smith-Dorrien's action as 'the ill-considered decision ... to give battle at Le Cateau'. But in truth, this small battle had been crucial to survival.

The Suffolk Memorial, (right) in an open field just to the west of Le Cateau, stands witness to the bravery and sacrifice of the 2nd Battalion, The Suffolk Regiment. It was here, on this exposed high ground, that the Suffolks endured repeated attacks from the enemy. They lost their Commanding Officer, were eventually surrounded, and when the remnants of the Battalion were finally mustered, only 2 officers and 111 other ranks were left, with 720 killed, wounded, or taken prisoner. The memorial marks the place where the Suffolks fought their last stand. They had played a crucial role in the battle and, after the war, Smith-Dorrien paid his tribute: '... had not the Suffolks and other intrepid troops refused to budge, there would have been nothing to prevent the enemy sweeping on the scattered units ... before they had time to get to the road allotted for their retirement. Had this happened, the safety of the whole force fighting at Le Cateau, and indeed the whole BEF, would have been jeopardized'.

VILLERS-COTTERETS FOREST OF RETZ

By the time 4th Guards Brigade reached the open ground just north of Villers-Cotterêts and the Forêt de Retz on the afternoon of 31st August, they had been marching for over a week, and it was here that they were ordered to halt and take up a hasty delaying position. The next morning the German advance guard arrived, and the battle that followed was short, sharp, extremely violent and, above all, confusing. Bullets ricocheted from trees and soldiers soon lost all sense of direction, and their units.

At the end of the fighting, the Guards had managed to delay the German advance, but at great cost. Some 90 officers and soldiers lay dead, and since this was a delaying action, there was no time to gather in the dead and lay them to rest. That task was left to the locals, who buried the soldiers in one single grave, in the centre of the forest and close to where they had fallen.

The following month, the mother of one of the young officers who was killed aged 18 returned to look for her son's grave. She could not find him, but a little later, the brother of the Irish Guards' Commanding Officer, also killed, was more successful. He found his brother's body, as well as the young officer's, identified by the initials on the back of his wrist-watch. In due course, the care of this beautiful and poignant cemetery was taken over by the Imperial War Graves Commission and named, 'Guards Grave'. Lady Edward Cecil, the young officer's mother, commissioned a simple private memorial to him and his fellow guardsmen; it now stands in the forest, not far from the cemetery.

> *"Hard pressed on my right. My centre is yielding.*
> *Impossible to manoeuvre. Situation excellent. I attack."*
>
> *Ferdinand Foch during the First Battle of the Marne, September 1914*

THE MIRACLE OF THE MARNE

The Battle of the Marne in mid-September 1914 brought the opening battles of manoeuvre to an end. The Germans had made impressive progress in August, following their plan to defeat the French in a matter of weeks before turning towards Russia. Paris, the final prize, seemed ready for the taking, and even the French government took the precaution of moving to Bordeaux. The reality was that all the armies were exhausted: the Germans had been on the advance since early August; and the Allies had been fighting one rearguard action after another.

With the Germans now close to Paris, Maréchal Joseph Joffre decided to make a stand south of the River Marne, by launching a counter-attack against the German First Army's right flank. When the Germans turned to meet this, a gap developed in their front line, an opportunity that Joffre was quick to exploit. With the support of the British, the French now began to drive a wedge into their enemy, but they were still not beaten. It was only the arrival of 6,000 French reservists from Paris, transported in many hundreds of taxi-cabs, followed by another French counter-attack, that finally tipped the balance and knocked the Germans back onto the defensive.

The Germans had now reached their culminating point, barely 30 miles from Paris. Their lines of communication were over extended, and the only option was to halt and regroup. Now it was the turn of the French and British to pursue their enemy. The advance was to be a slow one, and once the Germans reached the River Aisne, some 60 miles to the north, they stopped and established a defensive line.

The Battle of the Marne was indeed a miracle, and most of the credit was due to the French. The German offensive was over, some lost ground had been recovered, and their grand plans for a swift victory were in tatters. The human cost of the battle was high, and its long term consequence was to set the conditions for a static attritional war where holding a narrow but extended stretch of ground was to be the prevailing feature for nearly the next four years.

But at least the Germans had the relative luxury of retiring to ground of their own choosing before establishing their defensive positions. Where possible, they occupied the high ground, using all the natural defences afforded by the surrounding landscape and terrain. The French and British were less lucky, since they were forced to merely close up on the German defensive line, finding the best ground they could. Rarely was this ideal; low lying land was often layered in clay, where digging was easier but trenches less robust and drainage always a problem. In contrast, the German defences were well sighted and built, often deep into chalk uplands, and with a permanency that would have defied Allied logic. For the British and the French, trenches were an expedient. No one would win the war by occupying a long line of trenches; it was offensive action that would be decisive.

DETAIL OF THE MEMORIAL

Showing Maréchal Joffre, his hand upon the poor French poilu soldier, surrounded by his generals, with Field Marshal Sir John French, third from right.

THE MEMORIAL
AT MONDEMENT-MONTGIVROUX

Maréchal Joffre, commander of the French armies selected this spot some thirty miles south east of Paris just above the marshes of St Gond as the place to put this extraordinary memorial celebrating the 1st Battle of the Marne. It was here that the French turned onto the offensive defeating the exhausted German armies. Von Kluck's armies were to retreat and take up defensive positions on the River Aisne some sixty miles to the north.

THE GATES OF THE CHATEAU AT SOUPIR
ON THE RIVER AISNE

In early September, German Uhlans passed through the village of Soupir in pursuit of the French and British. Two weeks later, the Germans were back, following the Battle of the Marne, and this time with the Allies on their heels. During the last week in late September British soldiers marched through Soupir and onto the high ground above the village to find the Germans had halted and dug in along the Chemin des Dames, marking the beginning of trench warfare, an entirely different experience to the frenetic movement of the last two months. The Chateau, in the valley and south of the ridge, was destroyed in the war, leaving just the gates standing as a reminder of what happened here.

Next Page: VENDRESSE CEMETERY FROM THE
CHEMIN DES DAMES

It was on these slopes that trench warfare began. In September 1914, the Germans, having retreated from the Marne, decided to dig in and hold the ground on the Aisne. Now unable to advance further, the Allies had no option but to do the same. In October 1914 the British withdrew from the Chemin des Dames to redeploy in Ypres, and the French troops took over this sector.

YPRES & THE SALIENT

CLOTH HALL YPRES
Built at the turn of the 13th and 14th centuries, finished in 1304, and almost completely destroyed during the First World War, the Cloth Hall in Ypres was slowly reconstructed in the years that followed. In 1915, with its roof gone, it was a temporary haven for British troops as they waited to go up the line to the trenches. Before the war it had been the commercial hub of this busy merchant town. It is now occupied by the In Flanders Fields Museum.

YPRES

The Germans never managed to capture Ypres, although they had their chance on 7th October 1914 when a cavalry division swept through the town, taking bread for the soldiers, hay for their horses, and some 62,000 francs from the town's coffers. A few days later the British were to arrive in Ypres, and here they stayed for the remainder of the war while the fighting raged along the salient that surrounds the eastern and southern sides of the town.

Ypres was a key objective for both the Allies and the Germans, and now that it was held by the British, they were determined to hold at all costs the last bastion before the Channel ports. The first of four battles around Ypres took place in October and November 1914, when the Germans attempted to take the town that lay in their path to the coast. The British Expeditionary Force, often outnumbered, just managed to hold the line long enough for the German attack to falter and wane with the arrival of winter. But the battle that had all but destroyed the old regular British Army of August 1914 had only settled the matter of Ypres for the time being, doing nothing to bring to an end the Germans' desire to capture it.

The Germans, who often avoided big offensives, allowing the Allies to wear themselves down against their better and deeper defences, took a different approach at Ypres. Following their failure to break through in late 1914, they launched another big attack the following spring, in April 1915, when they used gas for the first time, and again in early 1918. For their part, the British, in an attempt to gain the high ground along the salient, attacked the Germans along the Messines Ridge in June 1917 and at Passchendaele a few months later. Although both sides experienced both tactical success and failure as a result of these offensives, ultimately nothing was decided here other than the status quo and a huge loss of life on both sides.

While the Germans had Ypres on a plate in October 1914, and very nearly captured the town in the spring of 1918, they ultimately failed to open up this vital route to the Channel ports. But where they did succeed was in the gradual and almost complete destruction of this beautiful and prosperous Flemish city. Many of the larger and grander buildings, such as the Cloth Hall and St Martin's Cathedral, were damaged by incendiaries in late 1914, but managed to remain partially standing for a while. During the Second Battle of Ypres in April 1915, the German bombardment intensified, and most of the civilians abandoned the town, with the remainder leaving the following month.

From then on, the town became a transitory but rarely safe resting place for British soldiers often en route to the front line, either to take their place in the trenches, or to carry out engineering work under the cover of darkness. By the end of the war, very little of the town remained standing, and with the total absence of civilians, it was perhaps not surprising, although rather misguided, for Winston Churchill to suggest that the town should remain as it was: 'I should like us to acquire the whole of the ruins of Ypres… a more sacred place for the British race does not exist in the world.'

Thankfully, the people of Ypres took their city back, and re-built it lovingly in an act of faith that endures to this day. The Cloth Hall stands again where it had been since the beginning of the 14th century, and the Cathedral is nearby. The locals also made room for a British presence that has provided a continuity since those dark days of the war. In July 1927, the Menin Gate, designed by Sir Reginald Blomfield, was inaugurated, bearing the names of more than 54,000 soldiers of the British Expeditionary Force who lost their lives in the Ypres Salient in the first three years of the war but for whom there is no known grave. It was Field Marshal Lord Plumer, in his address at that inauguration, who eloquently expressed the feelings of those relatives who now saw the names of their loved ones recorded on the panels of the memorial: 'and now it can be said of each one in whose honour we are assembled here today: He is not missing; he is here'.

"She was a city of patience; of proud name,
Dimmed by neglecting Time; of beauty and loss;
Of acquiescence in the creeping moss.
But on a sudden fierce destruction came
Tigerishly pouncing: thunderbolt and flame
Showered on her streets, to shatter them and toss
Her ancient towers to ashes. Riven across,
She rose, dead, into never-dying fame.
White against heavens of storm, a ghost, she is known
To the world's ends. The myriads of the brave
Sleep round her. Desolately glorified,
She, moon-like, draws her own far-moving tide
Of sorrow and memory; toward her, each alone,
Glide the dark dreams that seek an English grave."

'Ypres' by Lawrence Binyon

Left: THE MENIN GATE
Seen from outside the city walls

> *"It was simply the mud which defeated us ... The men did splendidly to get through it as they did. But the Flanders mud, as you know, is not a new invention. It has a name in history – it has defeated other armies before this one."*
>
> *Field Marshal Sir Douglas Haig*

FLANDERS MUD

Mud is an ubiquitous feature of war, but never more so than in Flanders where the two words have become synonymous. The high water table in this part of the Low Countries, appropriately named, and the systematic destruction of the irrigation systems that fed the fertile fields of the area, rendered the conditions here to be appalling beyond comprehension.

Ypres and the surrounding area lie on a flat plain consisting mainly of Ypres clay, similar to London clay. The resultant soil, when mixed with water, can produce a thick and glutinous mud which only becomes more ghastly in its consistency as it is disturbed and churned. In the early days, conditions could be deceptive; even where the ground appeared dry and when the sun was shining, hidden below this crust was a sodden mass just waiting to rise up. It might have survived the light passage of a few locals and horses, but not the weight of armies and high explosive.

By 1917, the battlefields of Flanders had been pounded by artillery and the topsoil had been stripped away. The landscape had become a bare and barren quagmire, something that no photograph of a muddy field today can replicate. Not only was the water rising from below, but also descending from above. In August 1917, rainfall was double the normal average, and October also proved to be an extremely wet month.

Movement to and from the battlefields, and living in damp water filled trenches, could be as challenging as the battles themselves; indeed, soldiers and horses could literally drown in the mud without any help from the enemy, and the fact that so many soldiers perished here without trace is due in part to these appalling conditions.

NIEUPORT MEMORIAL

The Nieuport Memorial stands in the Belgian coastal town of Nieuport, where the Western Front begins its long journey from the sea to the Alps. The memorial commemorates 566 Commonwealth officers and men killed on the Belgian coast during the First World War who have no known grave. Among them are 20 names of those who served with the Royal Naval Division during the siege of Antwerp in October 1914. The lions that stand at each of the three corners of the platform were designed by Charles Sargeant Jagger. Beyond is the memorial to King Albert I of the Belgians.

THE FATE OF BELGIUM

There are many visitors to Ypres, a beautiful town that has become something of a British shrine to the collective memory of the First World War. But it is important to remember that not just the British fought in Belgium and that, for most of the war, much of the country east of Ypres was occupied by the Germans. Following the invasion on 4th August 1914, civilians were routinely rounded up and selectively executed, and within four days around 850 had been murdered. It was a phenomenon that tragically often occurs when an invading army enjoys initial successes followed by stubborn resistance. The Germans saw the civilian population as their enemy, they imagined threats from all directions, and not just from the small and ill-equipped Belgian Army. There was a resentment towards the locals, fuelled by a general exhaustion among the German soldiers, the influence of alcohol, and ill-discipline. During the ten days of the main advance in late August, the Germans had crossed Belgium, killed civilians, destroyed villages, and deported some of the survivors. It was a brutal campaign, designed to stamp the invader's authority on a country that was merely a stepping-stone to France.

Belgium was ill-prepared, partly because of its neutral status and its belated attempt to create a modern army. With defence of its borders to the east relying almost entirely upon the great frontier forts of Liège and Namur, Belgium was quickly overwhelmed by the German army, numerically far superior and equipped with heavy artillery. The Belgian Army tried its best, but never stood a chance, being unable to hold territory or launch effective counter-attacks. Brussels was captured with hardly a shot fired, and the ease with which the capital city was occupied on 20th August was somehow symbolic of a hopeless endeavour on the part of the Belgian Army. As an American reporter, Richard Harding Davis, watching from the Hôtel de Ville in the Grand Place, observed: 'The entrance of the German army into Brussels has lost the human quality. It was lost as soon as the three soldiers who led the army bicycled into the Boulevard du Régent and asked the way to the Gare du Nord'.

With the frontier towns and Brussels in enemy hands, the port of Antwerp continued to be held by a Belgian garrison, later with some British support. By the end of September, the German bombardment began, but over the next ten days the Germans made inroads, and on 9th October the garrison surrendered. By now, just a tiny corner of Belgium remained, with a short length of the Western Front running from the French border to the sea. Ypres was at the axis of this defence, but there was still 20 miles of low-lying, completely flat and unforgiving ground that needed to be defended, a place where armies generally do not like to fight. It was here that the Belgian Army held the front line In October and November 1914, flooding parts of the surrounding countryside as a last-ditch attempt to prevent the Germans from capturing the Channel ports. Somehow it worked, and the German offensive moved south, where the First Battle of Ypres was about to take place. The area to the north was to be held by the Belgians for the remainder of the war, and although sporadic shelling continued, there was little movement along this sector.

TRENCH OF DEATH ON THE RIVER YSER

The 'Trench of Death' just to the south west of Diksmuide, has now been preserved in concrete. The apparent permanency of this place as a memorial is perhaps appropriate, since the Belgians continued to hold this stretch of the front line for over four years, despite being only 50 metres from a German bunker and under frequent fire from the enemy – hence the grim title. It is a place that has considerable symbolism in Belgium, since so many of the other monuments in this small country remember the soldiers of other nations.

SANCTUARY WOOD

This is an edgy place since it is quite unlike any other preserved or reconstructed trench-line along the Western Front. This is not part of a memorial park, and there are no neat pathways or grassed areas or information panels to explain what happened here. It has a dank feel about it, and one needs to walk carefully, looking out for angle-iron pickets protruding from the ground or the sharp corners of corrugated iron lining the trenches. What remains here of the war cannot be regarded as authentic in all respects, but standing in Sanctuary Wood in the half light of a late autumn afternoon, with a cold wind passing through the trees, looking at the slippery ground covered by fallen foliage and the occasional pile of rusty metal, can certainly play with one's imagination.

HOOGE CRATER

Unlike the 19 craters along the Messines Ridge, blown simultaneously as the opening gambit for a major offensive, the crater at Hooge was the consequence of a local difficulty. By the summer of 1915 the British position here was becoming untenable due to the Germans' commanding overview of the British front line. The solution was to dig tunnels underneath the German concrete fortifications along their front line and place a large mine there. When it was blown, at 7pm on 19th July 1915, the mine formed a crater some 120 feet wide and 20 feet deep, later captured by British soldiers. Now filled by water, the crater conveys a tranquillity far removed from the jagged and grotesque hole created in an instant in July 1915.

DETRITUS OF WAR – HOOGE

Sometimes just the sheer amount of metal and other man-made traces of war can defeat both the elements and the years that have passed by. Much of the ordnance and rusty barrels have disappeared, perhaps to a scrapyard, a museum, or a private collection. But evidence remains, sometimes below ground and revealed by the annual turning of soil, or hidden in the undergrowth of woods and forests. Barbed wire, and the simple but effective twisted stakes used to create obstacles to movement, were never easy to remove, and can still be found doing their job all these years later.

HOUSEHOLD CAVALRY AT THE FIRST BATTLE OF YPRES

The soldiers of the Household Cavalry had assumed their role in this war would be a mounted one, but their horses were soon to become a sad encumbrance since there was no role for them near the trenches. In his diary, Captain Sir Morgan Crofton, 2nd Life Guards, described his deep distress at the conditions they suffered. Tied up behind the lines for days on end, with only a few troopers to care for them, with no horse rugs, very little food, and in dismal weather, standing with their hocks in mud, it was a 'wretched existence that our horses were living'.

When the Germans attacked at the beginning of the First Battle of Ypres, it was the Household Cavalry's fate to be on the axis of the main advance, at Zandvoorde on the high ground south east of Ypres. Their trenches were makeshift, more like pits hastily dug in the sandy soil, and without the continuous zig-zag of later entrenchments that provided better protection and communications, both up to and along the line.

Early on 30th October 1914, 260 German guns opened up, shortly followed by an infantry assault of three Jäger battalions. It was to be a shattering day, with the loss of the ridge and the greater part of two squadrons. A second attack the following day, between Wytschaete and Messines, also took a heavy toll, with only remnants of the regiment left when the muster roll was taken. A third action, on 6th November, saw The Life Guards conducting a dismounted bayonet charge towards the Klein Zillebeke ridge to regain trenches abandoned earlier during a German attack. 2nd Lieutenant Howard Avenel Bligh St. George survived this attack, only to be killed nine days later. In a letter home he had described life at the front: 'We have been in the thick of it for the last four days, solid fighting day and night... You can't imagine what it's like. Words cannot describe the hell it is.'

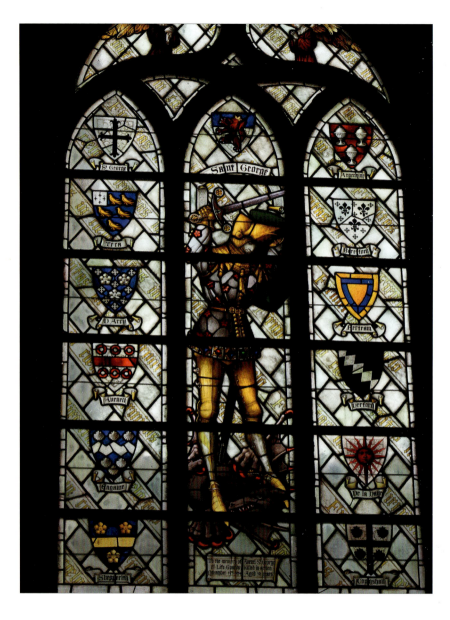

2ND LIEUTENTANT HOWARD AVENEL BLIGH ST GEORGE 1ST LIFE GUARDS

Howard Avenel Bligh St. George was killed by a sniper on 15th November 1914 aged just 19 years and is buried at Zillebeke Churchyard and commemorated by this stained glass window inside the church. In his last letter home to his parents, he wrote 'an awful lot of people are going home owing to their nerves going through constant shell fire. I admit it's trying. A lot of good fellows killed here in the last two days...'

The Memorial to the Household Cavalry in Belgium

This memorial stands on Zandvoorde Ridge, close to where the Household Cavalry were attacked in their trenches on 30th October 1914. The following day, a German officer came across the body of Lieutenant the Lord Worsley, Royal Horse Guards, who was killed there while commanding a machine-gun section. He was buried under a simple wooden cross, and after the war Worsley's widow purchased the land. His body was exhumed and moved to a military cemetery in Ypres in 1921, and the memorial was constructed at the same spot. It commemorates 120 men of the 1st Life Guards, 114 men of the 2nd Life Guards, and 62 men of the Royal Horse Guards, many of whom were killed holding the ridge at Zandvoorde.

*"It was here that the battle was won.
It was here that the battle and war
itself was very nearly lost."*

Lynn MacDonald, '1914; The Days of Hope'

BLACK WATCH CORNER, POLYGON WOOD

Some four miles east of Ypres, Polygon Wood and the surrounding area was almost continually fought over throughout the war. The memorial at Black Watch Corner, unveiled in 2014, stands on the edge of the wood and commemorates not only the desperate fighting that took place here in late 1914, but also the 8,960 Black Watch soldiers killed and 20,000 wounded during the First World War. On 11th November 1914, the Black Watch, Queen's Own Cameron Highlanders, and Scots Guards faced an attack by the Prussian Guards numbering some 17,500 men. These three regiments were all but wiped out, but the Germans never quite broke through. The Old Contemptibles had stood firm during the First Battle of Ypres. Had they failed, the Germans would almost certainly have broken through to the coast, cutting off the British Expeditionary Force entirely.

Opposite:
AUSTRALIAN MEMORIAL IN POLYGON WOOD

Here stands the memorial to the Australian 5th Division who cleared Polygon Wood at great cost during the Passchendaele battles of 1917. The remains of three German pillboxes captured by the Australians lie deep among the trees but few trench-lines remain. The Butte, an old rifle range, is still prominent and mounted on top is the AIF 5th Division memorial, an obelisk. In the foreground is the New Zealand Memorial commemorating the 378 New Zealanders killed in the Polygon Wood sector between September 1917 and May 1918 who have no known grave.

ESSEX FARM

A few days before the Second Battle of Ypres began in April 1915, the 1st Canadian Field Artillery Brigade took up a position here on the west bank of the canal. The brigade surgeon, Major John McCrae, had been an artillery officer in the Boer War, but was now serving as a doctor, spending 17 days at Essex Farm treating Canadians, British, Indians, French, and Germans. One death affected him profoundly. Lieutenant Alexis Helmer, a Canadian friend killed by a shell burst, was buried in the little cemetery next to the dressing station. McCrae performed the funeral ceremony and, the next day, wrote the poem 'In Flanders Fields'.

The poem was very nearly not published. Having completed it, McCrae threw the hand written page away, only for it to be retrieved by a fellow officer. It was published in 'Punch' in December 1915, and has become probably the most well-known poem of The Great War. Not only does it speak with the words of those soldiers who lie in Flanders Fields and, indeed, on other battlefields along the Western Front and elsewhere, it also provided the inspiration for the symbol of remembrance, the poppy. Looking back, it is perhaps not surprising that the poppy has become such an enduring emblem. Poppy seeds are disseminated by the wind, lying dormant on broken ground, waiting for the warm spring weather. When their buds open, the poppies flutter in the wind with their bright red colour, and while a field of poppies can radiate such a powerful presence, individually, they are fragile. Once picked, a poppy soon withers and dies.

In Flanders fields the poppies blow
Between the crosses, row on row,
That mark our place; and in the sky
The larks, still bravely singing, fly
Scarce heard amid the guns below.

We are the Dead. Short days ago
We lived, felt dawn, saw sunset glow,
Loved and were loved, and now we lie
In Flanders fields.

Take up our quarrel with the foe:
To you from failing hands we throw
The torch; be yours to hold it high.
If ye break faith with us who die
We shall not sleep, though poppies grow
In Flanders fields.

John McCrae

LANGEMARCK

There are not many German cemeteries along the Western Front, and the few that do exist can easily be overlooked among the many others that are such a feature. This was victor's justice imposed on a defeated enemy. Unlike the gifts of land 'in perpetuity' made willingly by the French and Belgian governments to their allies, the same generosity was never extended to nor sought by their old enemy.

Few German soldiers received the dignity of their own grave; many more were buried in massed graves, the Kameradengräber; some were returned to their homeland while a countless number have disappeared without trace. But tangible evidence of German casualties does remain, and Langemarck on the northern corner of the Ypres Salient is perhaps the most famous of all German First World War cemeteries, containing over 44,000 burials of which less than half are identified by name.

Langemarck has a dark and Wagnerian feel to it. Surrounded partly by a moat constructed in grey stone and incorporating the fortified bunkers built by the Germans for the later Ypres battles, it sits like a bastion fort in a foreign and alien land – a 'Totenburg' (fortress of the dead). After the war, the cemetery became a symbol for the German spirit, exemplified by the young students who willingly joined up in 1914 only to die a few months later in the so-called 'massacre of the innocents'. In the 1930s, the myth of Langemarck took on an even greater significance as a collective expression of National Socialism. In 'Mein Kampf' written a few years earlier, Adolf Hitler claimed that he had fought here (he did not), and in 1940 he visited the cemetery and other places on the Ypres Salient.

Next page: LANGEMARCK CEMETERY AT DAWN

MESSINES

The Battle of Messines is remembered particularly for the devastating manner in which it opened at 03:10 in the early hours of 7th June 1917. Meticulously planned over many months, requiring the extensive digging of tunnels across No Man's Land and the laying of massive mines under the German positions, the battle began with simultaneous explosions that almost certainly generated the loudest man-made bang hitherto in history. The night before the battle, General Sir Herbert Plumer said wryly to his staff 'Gentlemen, we may not make history tomorrow, but we shall certainly change the geography'; while the next morning, it is said, the Prime Minister, David Lloyd George, heard the explosion in Downing Street.

19 mines exploded, and while any element of surprise for the subsequent infantry advance was now well and truly lost, this was easily offset by this massive explosion that did indeed change the shape of the Messines-Wytschaete ridge. The effect on the Germans was utterly devastating. Some 10,000 men were killed in that split second of explosive energy, and as the 'pillar of fire' dimmed and the debris came back to earth, thousands of British infantrymen surged forward under a creeping artillery barrage and supported by tanks and gas attacks directly into the German trenches.

Despite the barbaric and primeval way the battle opened, many aspects of its detail characterised a future way of war. Lessons from recent battles were acknowledged. For example, the effectiveness of artillery support had been improved by the use of highly accurate maps, field survey, gun calibration, and calculations based on the effects of weather. Sound-ranging equipment was used to identify enemy artillery positions; some 90% of them had already been found even before the battle had started. Good communications were what made it all possible – the use of radio and telephone lines dug deep below ground.

The battle was short, sharp, and successful for the British. The first objectives were taken within three hours, and the remainder by mid-afternoon. The Germans counter-attacked the following day, losing further ground. They attacked repeatedly for the next four days, by which time all of Messines Ridge had been captured by the British. The battle was one of the most successful operations of the war, and although casualties were heavy on both sides, it proved that, with careful planning and ruthless execution, an attacker could prevail over a well-protected defender.

Messines is now a tranquil place. Many of the craters remain in the soft and richly arable fields and are now filled with water. Although man-made by massive explosions from below rather than gentle excavation from above, they appear entirely natural, an almost integral part of the landscape.

POOL OF PEACE, SPANBROEKMOLEN

Next page: KRUISSTRAAT DOUBLE CRATER

Above: RESTORED GERMAN TRENCHES AT BAYERNWALD (BAVARIAN WOOD), *so named by Bavarian soldiers in late 1914. Adolf Hitler served here as a runner in 1914, and this is where he won his Iron Cross. The cemetery is near to the site of an old chapel that was painted by Hitler when he was here. In June 1940, following the conquest of Belgium, Hitler returned to the Ypres Salient to visit some familiar places along the line.*

Left: CROONAERT CHAPEL CEMETERY
Looking out from the Bayernwald Ridge towards Croonaert Chapel Cemetery.

PROWSE POINT CEMETERY

A unique cemetery on the Ypres Salient, since it is named after an individual. It is where the Hampshire Regiment and the Somerset Light Infantry fought bravely in October 1914, an action in which Major Charles Prowse displayed particular courage. Prowse later became a brigadier-general and was killed on 1st July 1916, the first day of the Battle of the Somme. Not far from the cemetery, seen here from Ploegsteert Wood in winter sunshine, is the front line from where the Christmas Truce took place in 1914.

HILL 60 YPRES

Hill 60 began life as a man-made heap of earth excavated from the cutting of the Ypres-Comines railway. Forming an area of high ground during the First Battle of Ypres, it quickly became an objective worth acquiring. The Germans seized the hill in November 1914, and managed to hold it until April 1915.

It is not so much what happened on the surface of this strange and unnatural feature that defines it, but what occurred deep below the ground. A labyrinth of tunnels had been built by the opposing armies during the lead-up to the big battle in 1915, and with the help of subterranean mines exploded beneath the German lines, the British took Hill 60 relatively easily, while inflicting huge loss of life on their enemy. But the hill formed its own salient and became impossible to hold. The Germans recaptured it, and so the mining and counter mining continued until the Battle of Messines, with its vast and simultaneous explosions along the front line, finally settled the matter.

Nearly 100 years on, and Hill 60 remains a monstrous man-made mound of uneven and pock-marked ground and disturbed looking concrete, albeit now covered with grass, bushes and some trees. Unlike the craters along the Messines front, with their almost natural and circular form, Hill 60 is something of an ugly and disturbing aberration.

Next Page: ## CATERPILLAR CRATER

The original Caterpillar was a mound of earth, a by-product of the railway cutting that runs between here and Hill 60, so named due to its caterpillar shape. But the effect of the vast mine that exploded below ground here was to entirely remove the feature that once stood here, creating a perfectly formed crater that is now filled with water. The trees and the path that runs around this large pool give an entirely peaceful and tranquil feel to this place, and it seems almost impossible that this could have been formed as the result of one massive explosion. A more detailed story of what actually happened here is probably hidden in the collapsed and flooded tunnels that lie beneath this crater, just one example of another vast and complex landscape that exists below ground, here and elsewhere along the Western Front. Very little of it has been explored; most of it never will be.

THE ZIEGLER BUNKER

One of the best preserved bunkers on the Western Front, this one near Boezinge has also been described as the 'Viking Ship'. The bunker was constructed by the German Army and later captured by the French.

I died in hell –
(They called it Passchendaele).

Siegfried Sassoon

TYNE COT CEMETERY

Much has been written about Tyne Cot Cemetery, the largest
Commonwealth War Graves Cemetery in the world. It was constructed
on the very site of battle, incorporating German bunkers captured by
Australian soldiers. There are many unknown graves here, reflecting the
appalling conditions and the extent to which the Flanders mud literally
consumed the dead. Tyne Cot is also where the names of the Missing
of the Ypres Salient, those who died in the later battles and who do not
appear on the other similar memorials nearby, are recorded. But leaving
aside the cemetery itself and the memorials, this place also demonstrates
something else about the salient and its proximity to Ypres. Stand here,
somewhere in the centre of the cemetery, on the old German front line,
and look towards the city, just over five miles away. There is nothing
particularly prominent about the ground over which these battles were
fought, but it is higher than the city. For much of the war, the Germans
occupied this dominating position, and while they never managed to
capture Ypres, it is not surprising that they were able to destroy so much
of it by artillery fire.

Next Page **TYNE COT CEMETERY**
There are 11,962 Commonwealth servicemen of The Great War buried
here, together with the names of nearly 35,000 servicemen from the
United Kingdom and New Zealand who died after 17th August 1917
and have no known grave.

THE ARTOIS

THE BATTLES OF 1915 AND 1917

There are many similarities between Arras and Ypres. Both were variously the centres of the wool trade, and their Flemish style of architecture is similar, each with their 'Grand Place' and public buildings. They lay very close to the front line, were bombarded with artillery, and gradually reduced to rubble. In the aftermath, both were slowly rebuilt to the extent that their apparent continuity seems to have been untouched by time, save for the memorials and cemeteries that are now such a feature of the urban landscape.

In late August 1914, German Uhlans appeared in Arras, to be followed by a German garrison taking up residence in the citadel. By early October, the French had regained possession, and the Allies were to hold the town for the remainder of the war. But more importantly, the Germans had seized the high ground to the north-east, dominating Arras and much of the surrounding countryside, ground over which the war was to be fought for much of the next three years.

In late 1914, there was a short lull in Artois during the closing few weeks of November, as the Western Front took shape and the German attacks around the Ypres Salient tailed off. Then, just a few days before Christmas, the first of three Allied offensives in Artois began; it lasted until mid-January, ending in stalemate.

In May 1915, following the opening of the Second Battle of Ypres a few weeks earlier, the French began another offensive in Artois, aimed in part at cutting the German lines of communication that supplied the area east of Arras and Rheims. With the support of the British along Aubers Ridge to the north, the

French captured Vimy Ridge but were then pushed back by German counter-attacks. The British attack also ended in failure, although later at Festubert they gained some ground and a brief respite for the French. The joint offensive lingered on until late June 1915, with only modest gains for the Allies and huge losses on both sides.

The third Artois offensive came in September 1915, at a time when the Allies' failure to make any progress along the Western Front was becoming a critical concern. This next offensive, the 'Big Push', was somehow seen as possibly the last, and hopefully the best, chance of forcing a decisive result before the odds began to turn against the Allies. This would be a large-scale operation, with simultaneous offensives in the Champagne region, with one senior British commander predicting that the forthcoming battle would be 'the greatest battle in the history of the world'.

Maréchal Joffre was hopeful that the Germans might be pushed back as far as the Meuse. British commanders were less optimistic, since the ground that they had been allocated was unfavourable for an attack, a bleak and flat landscape in a coalmining region, with no cover anywhere. Sir Douglas Haig was worried about the lack of artillery and shells, predicting that the enemy would have all the advantages. Sir John French acquiesced to Joffre's requests for support, and Kitchener made it clear that this attack must go forward, regardless. Allied solidarity was paramount, and Kitchener reluctantly committed two divisions of his New Army. This offensive came at a moment of crisis for the Allies, with France's massive losses during the first six months of the war and the widespread destruction of the old BEF. Many of the old regulars were dead, and the war would now be fought by war-time soldiers: reservists, volunteers, and, from early 1916, conscripts.

The Allied artillery barrage began on 21st September 1915 and four days later the infantry advanced from their trenches. On the British sector at Loos, Haig ordered the release of gas, but the wind left gas clouds hanging in No Man's Land as the infantry advanced, causing some casualties. Despite this, there were some early successes as German trenches were overrun. But their real strong points were not in the front line and the Allied infantry were being drawn forward to where they could neither sustain a fight nor be reinforced from the rear. The offensive soon became bogged down, and Joffre finally called a halt on 30th September, making just one last abortive attempt to seize Vimy Ridge ten days later. It had been another bitter failure, as both the Allies and Germans struggled to achieve the elusive and decisive breakthrough. They did not find the answer in 1915.

1916 was a relatively quieter time in the Artois sector, although there was one short battle in mid-July, at Fromelles, intended as a diversionary attack to draw the Germans away from the Somme where a major Allied offensive had begun on 1st July. British and Australian troops attacked the Germans following a short and intensive artillery preparation, but the operation was based on faulty intelligence and was a disaster with very heavy casualties, particularly among the Australians.

The Battle of Arras, in April 1917, part of the wider, and much less successful Nivelle Offensive, was an opportunity to apply some of the many lessons of trench warfare. The British plan was to attack on a frontage of 11 miles, between Vimy Ridge and Neuville-Vitasse, four miles south of the Scarpe River. There was to be a prolonged bombardment prior to the assault, and when the infantry advanced, units would leapfrog forward in order to maintain momentum. The whole operation was supported by considerable preparation which included a detailed fire-plan employing a creeping barrage ahead of the advancing infantry. The existing network of old caverns and underground quarries under Arras was pressed into service, with new tunnels dug to link them up and as a way to get the assaulting troops close to the front line in relative safety. Mines were also placed below the German front line, ready to be detonated at Zero Hour.

The infantry assault began on 9th April 1917 in appalling weather conditions. At Vimy Ridge, the Canadians took all their objectives in a matter of hours, while the British had some success further south. Over the next few days, the Germans were pushed back from their front line trenches and in some places gains of some three miles were achieved, despite strong counter-attacks. Thereafter, the battle became a slogging match which continued until 23rd May when the Nivelle Offensive ended. The BEF suffered 158,660 casualties while the Germans lost between 130,000 and 160,000 killed and wounded.

For the British and Canadians the battle is remembered mainly for the capture of Vimy Ridge, and although little changed along the Western Front as a result, Vimy became a particularly important and symbolic victory for the Canadians since, in many ways, it was their victory. The town of Arras also benefited; for the first time in the war the front line was no longer immediately on its doorstep.

THE INDIAN ARMY AT NEUVE CHAPELLE

The Indian Expeditionary Force, with two infantry divisions and two cavalry divisions, arrived in France in late September 1914. Still wearing their lightweight khaki drill uniforms, and now equipped with the latest pattern Enfield rifle with which they had received hardly any training, the Indians were soon in action on the Ypres Salient. They were good soldiers from the martial races, Sikhs, Pathans, Dogras, Jats, and Rajputs, as well as Gurkhas from Nepal, but they were now fighting in unfamiliar surroundings, without warm clothing, and in appalling weather conditions. They had trained for an entirely different type of colonial warfare, where stealth, ambushes, patrolling, and fieldcraft were the key skills. Now they were expected to fight from waterlogged trenches, in a war of heavy artillery, machine-gun fire, mortars, and gas attacks. Not surprisingly, morale was not good.

The Indians fought in numerous actions in those early months, and on 10th March 1915 were in the front line at Neuve Chapelle for the first major British offensive of the war. The battle began with a short and intensive artillery bombardment and then, in damp misty conditions, the British and Indian infantry attacked across a two mile frontage. The village of Neuve Chapelle was quickly captured and German trenches overrun. But there had been problems with the British guns, and some of the Indian units had no supporting artillery fire at all. A German counter-attack was repulsed two days later but British artillery supplies were by now running low, and the offensive was abandoned on 13th March. There were 7,000 British and 4,200 Indian casualties at Neuve Chapelle, and the battle had demonstrated some of the challenges of trench warfare, the importance of good planning, surprise, artillery support, and good communications. While the battle proved that breakthroughs were possible, exploiting success was a much harder task. It would take many battles before all these lessons were fully learned and applied.

The Indians suffered more casualties during the Second Battle of Ypres in late April 1915 when the Germans used chlorine gas for the first time. Ill-prepared for this new ghastly form of warfare, the Indians' morale was now at a low point, not helped by the heavy casualties among their British officers, since their replacements could not speak their language and knew nothing of their cultural differences.

"I saw them – I can see them now – shivering in those early and primitive trenches, standing up to their knees in foul water. Their features composed in that mask of fatalism which gave an impression of pathos altogether terrible. Their bodies were often broken by the elements, but their souls were never conquered."

Lord Birkenhead, at the unveiling of the Neuve Chapelle memorial, 1927

The Indian infantry fought again at Loos in September 1915, and were later withdrawn to serve in Egypt, Palestine, Gallipoli, Mesopotamia, and East Africa. The Indians had provided invaluable service on the Western Front, and it is a tribute to them that they fought so well, and in a theatre of war for which they were not well-suited. One of the Indians' particular legacies to the British derived from years of colonial skirmishing: the art of patrolling. This skill was to become an invaluable part of trench warfare, helping to maintain fighting spirit during the quieter months between big offensives while dominating No Man's Land, probing the enemy, and finding out where his trenches lay.

Some 140,000 Indians served on the Western Front, 90,000 as combatants and 50,000 as labourers, with an officer corps that was mostly British. Over 8,550 soldiers were killed and some 50,000 were wounded, and of these, nearly 5,000 have no known grave and are commemorated on the Menin Gate at Ypres and on the Indian Memorial at Neuve Chapelle.

MEMORIAL TO THE INDIAN FALLEN
AT NEUVE CHAPELLE

THE BATTLEFIELD OF LOOS

Loos remains a stark and bare place, where the only features are slag heaps from the coalmines and the occasional rickety-looking pithead tower. The battle in September 1915 had begun well for the British but ended with only limited gains that failed to justify the casualties sustained. Rudyard Kipling's son Jack was lost at Loos, and he later vainly toured the field hospitals in the hope of finding him alive. After the war, in his description of the Battle of Loos, Kipling wrote: 'So, when the Press was explaining to a puzzled public what a far reaching success had been achieved, the "greatest battle in the history of the world" simmered down to picking up the pieces on both sides of the line, and a return to autumnal trench-work, until more and heavier guns could be designed and manufactured in England. Meanwhile, men died.'

AUSTRALIAN WAR MEMORIAL FROMELLES

There have been many new memorials in France and Flanders in recent years, and this one at Fromelles is particularly significant since it marks the first action fought by the Australians on the Western Front. The battle, which began on the early evening of 19th July 1916, was intended to distract the Germans from the major offensive on the Somme that had begun on 1st July but was now faltering badly. A long artillery bombardment removed the element of surprise as the Australian and British attackers at Fromelles came up against German machine-gunners in well defended positions. While there were some local successes during the battle, these could not be sustained. By the following morning the battle was over, with 5,500 Australian and 1,550 British casualties. The attack had failed completely.

The Memorial Park at Fromelles was opened in 1998. 10 years later, in 2008, the bodies of 250 Australian and British soldiers were discovered in mass graves in a wood just outside Fromelles; they had all been killed during the battle in July 1916. Their remains were exhumed, with some of the Australian bodies later being identified by DNA analysis. A new military cemetery was dedicated on 19th July 2010, the anniversary of the Battle of Fromelles.

Next Page: ## NOTRE-DAME-DE-LORRETTE

The military cemetery at Notre-Dame-de-Lorette, the largest French military cemetery in the world, is just three miles from Vimy Ridge and clearly visible from the main autoroute that sweeps down from Calais to Arras and beyond. Like Vimy it is on the high ground that was of huge tactical significance during the First World War, hence the monuments. The cemetery here contains the remains of some 40,000 Frenchmen, of whom 23,000 lie in seven ossuaries. The Byzantine-style basilica and the lantern tower with its magnificent view across the battlefield were built in the 1920s, and at the base of the tower is an ossuary containing the bones of 6,000 soldiers. The whole sense and feel of this place, as with all other French military cemeteries, are entirely different to the Commonwealth cemeteries. They need to be visited.

MUSLIM GRAVES AT NOTRE-DAME-DE-LORETTE

Here lie the graves of Muslim soldiers from the 1st Moroccan Division, with each headstone facing east. These soldiers, from former French territories in North Africa, fought along the high ground here and at Vimy during the battles of 1915.

Opposite: VIMY RIDGE

The Canadian National Vimy Memorial at Vimy Ridge, Canada's largest overseas national memorial, is a remarkable structure and quite distinct in design from any other along the Western Front. Although so prominent on the high ground, it can easily be missed by the traveller rushing along the autoroute that passes less than a mile to the west. Plantations shield a wider view of the monument when seen from afar, while the occasional flash of brilliantly white Seget limestone is revealed fleetingly along the fire breaks in the trees. Once beyond the forest, the visitor can appreciate the full grandeur of this monument as it stands on the highest point of the ridge, looking out across the Douai Plain. It was designed by the Canadian sculptor and designer Walter Seymour Allward, took 11 years to construct, and was unveiled in 1936. More recently, it has been extensively renovated and looks like a new structure on the landscape.

Next page: VIMY RIDGE AT DUSK

This elevated photograph shows how Vimy Ridge dominates the area, looking down onto the industrial area of the Lens-Douai plain.

TRENCHES AT VIMY

Vimy Ridge was seized by the Germans in September 1914, and they were determined to hold it, building deep defensive positions that would make it almost impossible to be captured. It dominated the surrounding landscape, overlooking Lens-Douai to the east and Arras to the south, allowing the Germans to shell the town at will. Despite costly attempts by the French in 1915 to capture the high ground, it remained firmly in German hands. In 1916, the Arras sector passed to the British, but the problem of Vimy was not to be resolved until the following year when, in April 1917, the Canadian Corps was given the task of capturing it. Following meticulous training and preparation and a well-coordinated British artillery barrage that endured for three weeks, four Canadian divisions attacked on 9th April. Within an hour, the first and second line of German trenches were captured, and by 12th April the battle was effectively over when Hill 145, the highest point on the ridge, fell. The victory was the greatest Allied success of the war so far, and it was almost entirely a Canadian operation.

Vimy Ridge continues to have immense symbolism for Canada, with an army that had barely existed before 1914. The victory was a defining event. To quote Brigadier-General Alexander Ross: 'in those few minutes I witnessed the birth of a nation'. The victory emboldened the Canadian government, and the country no longer saw itself as merely a British dominion, but a nation in its own right.

The preserved trenches at the Vimy Memorial Park are perhaps the most well known of any along the Western Front, and their preservation dates back to 1922 when the Canadian Government was granted ownership of the land by France. The battlefield was cleared of debris and ordnance, although some of this remains buried to this day, and the decision was taken to keep the wartime landscape, with its trenches, bunkers, tunnels, and craters. This place is now a memorial park, and its depiction as a battlefield has become stylised, although it does have an invaluable historical value, by conveying a sense of scale and proportion.

This is no longer a stark ridgeline with no ground cover or trees. It's a well-cared-for park, landscaped and grassed, with neat paths, fences, and information boards. The forests that surround Vimy, all replanted in the intervening years, give the place a kind of 'Sunday afternoon' feel. Local cyclists, runners and walkers are frequent visitors. Coach loads of school children, mostly British, are seen here during the week. Young Canadian students, extremely well trained and knowledgeable, shepherd visitors around the trenches and through the tunnels below and to the visitor centre. As an experience, Vimy is very different to other battlefield sites along the Western Front, many of which remain hidden and unfamiliar to the casual passer-by.

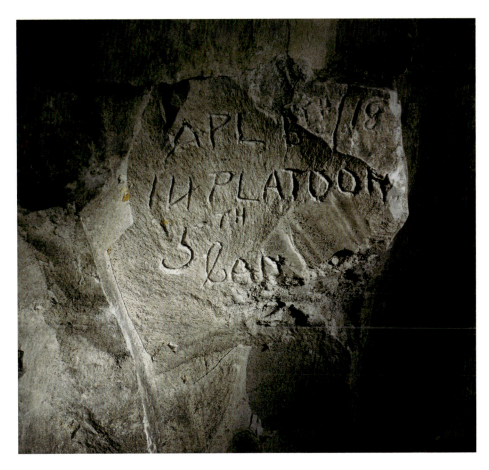

Above: GRAFFITI
Scrawled into the soft limestone by Canadian Troops.

CARRIÈRE WELLINGTON

Now part of a museum below Arras, La Carrière Wellington was opened in 2008 to remember the many soldiers who were here and, in particular, the New Zealand tunnellers who arrived in March 1916 to dig a network of tunnels that linked the old tunnels and underground quarries below the town. It is along these tunnels that many soldiers made their way forward to the front line for the big offensive that began on 9th April 1917.

POINT DU JOUR MEMORIAL AND CEMETERY
On 9th April 1917, as part of the Battle of Arras, the 9th (Scottish) Division captured German positions around Point du Jour. This cairn, constructed with stone from Scotland, commemorates the men and units that served with the 9th Division during the war. In 2006 the Commonwealth War Graves Commission moved the memorial to a new site close to the Point du Jour Military Cemetery.

Next page: ## BATTERY VALLEY
Once the attack was started, the British infantry of the 12th (Eastern) Division made spectacular advances. Houdain Cemetery can be seen on the ridge and it was from close to here that the soldiers of the 5th Royal Berkshire Regiment swept down to capture the German artillery gun-line concealed in the bottom of the valley. These guns were then turned round and used on the retreating enemy.

89

THE VIEW FROM ORANGE HILL CEMETERY

Arras is now much bigger than it was during the First World War,
although from here the Hôtel de Ville can still be seen clearly in the
centre of the town, three and a half miles west of Orange Hill Cemetery.
When the 1917 Arras offensive began on 9th April, the front line ran
through the fields that are now built up in the outskirts of the town. By
15th April, the whole of this landscape, to a depth of over three miles,
had been captured by the British, the furthest advance anywhere on
the Western Front to date. Arras was never far away, and still in range
of German artillery, but it was a little safer. Orange Hill was reached on
10th April 1917, was recaptured by the Germans in March 1918, and
then taken back in August. Bunyans Cemetery, where 53 soldiers killed in
1917 are buried, can just be seen to the left of the road, in the middle
distance.

THE MEMORIAL TO THE 37TH ENGLISH DIVISION

The 37th Division, a New Army Division consisting mostly of regiments from the Midlands, captured the village of Monchy-le-Preux on 11th April 1917 during the Battle of Arras. Although it commemorates the action here that day, this fine memorial records the units and battle honours of the division throughout its time on the Western Front. The memorial stands on the high ground in the village, looking out across the old battlefield to the east of Arras.

Left: MONCHY-LE-PREUX

A view from the west of Monchy Cemetery looking towards Monchy-le-Preux, one of the final objectives during the Battle of Arras. Designed by Sir Edwin Lutyens, the cemetery contains 581 burials of those British and Canadians killed here in 1917 and 1918.

THE SOMME

THE SOMME

The Somme is a mostly agricultural region of France which, in many ways, looks like parts of Southern England: gently rolling landscapes, fields of mixed arable and grazing, interspersed with woods, copses and villages. Perhaps the most obvious difference is that farmhouses and buildings here are either in or on the outskirts of the villages while in England they can be more isolated and out in the countryside. The view from the high ground is often a wide rural vista interrupted not by the farm buildings and barns that one would expect but by the cemeteries that lie out in the fields.

The Somme will be forever associated with the First World War, and above all, it is the tragedy of the opening day of the battle on 1st July 1916, when over 19,000 soldiers of the Third and Fourth British Armies were killed or died of their wounds, that dominates much of the story. But the battle was not just a British one. Alongside the English, Scots, Irish and Welsh, there were Australians, New Zealanders, Canadians, and Newfoundlanders. And there had been the French during the early months of the war on the flank of the British in 1916, and the Germans since October 1914. The battle in 1916 was to endure for over four months, and for the British it lingers in the collective memory just in the same way as Verdun does for the French. 1st July 1916 still manages to invoke disbelief and horror, compounding all those notions of incompetent generals, lions led by donkeys, the bravery of the rank and file, and the

dreadful futility of it all. Most visitors to the Somme battlefield come for perhaps two or three days, and in a symbolic way rarely make it far beyond the 1st July front-line trenches.

There had been fighting here in the autumn of 1914 as the French and Germans tried to outmanoeuvre each other. As both began to falter through exhaustion, the Germans had the advantage of choosing good positions from which to defend their territorial gains. While their grand plans had gone awry, the Germans north of the meandering River Somme were at least able to secure the high ground from where they could dominate the landscape and their enemy, the French. It was probably only in early 1917 when the Germans abandoned the Somme battlefield altogether, that the Allies were able to fully appreciate just how good their enemy's defences had been here. Not only did they dig deep into the chalk, constructing excellent underground bunkers, living quarters, and well-protected machine-gun posts, they also used the hamlets and villages as an integral part of their forward defences. During the Battle of the Somme many of those place names were to become well-known back home: Gommecourt, Serre, Beaumont Hamel, Thiepval, La Boisselle, Fricourt, Mametz and Mountauban. They had been British objectives during the battle, and were all eventually captured and largely destroyed in the process. Then later, they became battle honours, recorded on memorials both on the Somme and in other faraway places across the British Empire.

HAWTHORN RIDGE NO 2. CEMETERY
There are over 200 soldiers buried in this cemetery in the Newfoundland Memorial Park and in No Man's Land. Almost all who are buried here died on 1st July 1916, and some 50 graves are unidentified. This cemetery has a special intimacy, since its gravestones touch each other. The soldiers fought together, and now they lie shoulder-to-shoulder in long burial trenches.

"The Somme was the muddy grave of the German Field Army"

Hauptmann von Henig
German Guard Reserve Divsion

THIEPVAL MEMORIAL FROM THE WEST
Seen from across the Ancre valley, the German front line was astride the ridge where the Thiepval Memorial now stands. The British trenches were on the damp and muddy slopes along the edge of the wood.

"I have a rendezvous with Death
At some disputed barricade,
When Spring comes back with rustling shade
And apple-blossoms fill the air—
I have a rendezvous with Death
When Spring brings back blue days and fair."

Alan Seeger

The Somme had been a quiet sector when the British began to arrive here in the late summer of 1915, and was to remain so throughout the winter and into the following year. The comparisons with Flanders and the Ypres Salient were stark for those soldiers who had fought there. The Somme seemed somehow safer, retaining a few of the qualities of a peacetime landscape, albeit one that was now occupied by two large opposing armies. Many of the villages remained intact and still occupied by the locals. Farmers continued to farm their land, while woods and forests provided some cover on the front line and in the rear areas.

Everything began to change in late June 1916 when a monstrous artillery barrage started as the preparation for the big Allied offensive. It was to continue for a week, with some 1.6 million shells being fired onto the German positions. Expectations were high, with a hope that the infantry advance through the remains of the enemy trenches and strongpoints would be rapid. But it was not to be. The artillery barrage had failed; many of the shells did not explode, and those that did caused less damage than hoped. The Germans were prepared and waiting, deep in their well-protected bunkers and dug-outs. When the British artillery stopped and the infantry left their trenches to walk across No Man's Land, it was the signal for the Germans to emerge and man their trenches and machine-gun posts. From here they were well placed to defend their positions, and although the attackers achieved some limited tactical gains on the first day, there were to be no breakthroughs and casualties were high.

The British had no real choice but to continue the battle as best they could, since there were bigger strategic issues at play. The first day had been a failure, but there was a need to keep trying. The offensive was relaunched, tactics were modified, and more soldiers were committed to battle. Slowly, very slowly, the British crept forward, but this was not the kind of battle that anyone had expected. In September there was a renewed hope of a breakthrough with the introduction of tanks, but there were too few of these experimental machines, and they were mechanically unreliable. The following month there were torrential rains, and much of the battlefield became a quagmire with a thick and glutinous consistency of chalk and clay that clung to men's boots and clothes, dragging them down.

The battle finally ended on 18th November 1916, not with a decisive victory or defeat, but because of harsh weather and general exhaustion. Over the past four and a half months, the Allies and the Germans had suffered over 1.2 million casualties. The tactical gains had been insignificant, about five miles. But despite the huge human sacrifice, the Battle of the Somme did at least achieve something. It provided a little relief for the French at Verdun, the British learnt hard lessons which they were to apply to later battles, and it encouraged the Germans to avoid such battles ever again.

THE AMERICAN POET ALAN SEEGER
Seeger kept his appointment with death on 4th July 1916. Living in Paris on the outbreak of war, he volunteered for service with the French Foreign Legion. He was killed in the French sector, south of the River Somme.

HAWTHORN RIDGE

A view from Hawthorn Ridge that could so easily be Wiltshire or Hampshire farmland but for the three war cemeteries that lie across the landscape. Their position says much for the topography of the Battle of the Somme, for they are in No Man's Land and almost equidistant from the old British and German front lines. It was here that soldiers fell, and it is here that they are buried.

On the right, and just a few yards from the modern camera's lens, a mine laid 75 feet below the earth was exploded by the British at 07:20 hours on the morning of 1st July 1916. The timing of the explosion remains controversial, since the local commander ordered the mine to be blown some eight minutes ahead of others along the front line. The element of surprise was sacrificed by this odd decision and, tragically, casualties on this sector were particularly heavy, and for no gains whatsoever.

The explosion is memorable for another reason: it was filmed by Geoffrey Malins, one of the very few official British photographers on the Western Front during the First World War. Malins, with his wooden boxed and hand-cranked camera, was just

over 300 yards from the explosion, gripping his tripod as 'The ground where I stood gave a mighty convulsion. Then for all the world like a gigantic sponge, the earth rose high in the air to the height of hundreds of feet'. The flickering images of that remarkable film footage show an almost perfectly elliptical eruption of energy, just as Malins describes.

The crater is now surrounded by trees and hawthorn bushes, and is very different in appearance to other large craters along the Western Front, since a second mine was blown here on 13th November 1916 during the last few days of the Battle of the Somme. In a strange way, this second explosion has served to help blend this deep man-made creation into the surrounding landscape. Look inside, through the trees, and it does not really look like a crater at all, just an uneven, craggy, and massive hole in the ground. But contrast this with John Masefield's description in 1917, conveying an ugly rawness, now softened by time and undergrowth… 'The inside has rather the look of meat, for it is reddish and all streaked and scabbed with this pox and with discoloured chalk. A lot of it trickles and oozes like sores discharging pus, and this liquid gathers in holes near the bottom, and is greenish and foul and has the look of dead eyes staring upwards'.

SERRE

Serre is very much the story of the volunteer 'Pals' battalions that formed part of Kitchener's New Army. The manner in which these mostly young men so willingly joined up is described by the historian John Keegan as 'a spontaneous and genuinely popular mass movement which has no counterpart in the modern, English speaking world and perhaps could have none outside its own time and place'. They joined up together because they knew each other, worked together, joined the same sporting clubs, and often lived in the same streets. Serving together in the Army was an immediate attraction since it mirrored the friendships and relationships of the pre-war Edwardian era. But since these men went into action together, many died together, and are now buried close to where they fell. Perhaps it was as they wished; if one was to fight, better to do it surrounded by friends and comrades. But for the families back home it was to have a shattering impact on small communities.

The attack of the 'Pals' battalions faltered, as elsewhere on the Somme, when the infantry climbed from their trenches to face German machine-gun fire and artillery. These small cemeteries, neat and tidy, looking like small English urban gardens, stride out across No Man's Land in defiance of the enemy that has long since disappeared.

BEAUMONT HAMEL & NEWFOUNDLAND PARK MEMORIAL

Probably one of the most visited places along the Somme, and one of the most easily recognisable, is a preserved stretch of the battlefield where the Newfoundland Regiment attacked on 1st July 1916 in a tragic and costly attempt to take the heavily defended village of Beaumont Hamel beyond. In the early post-war days, both before and after the opening of the memorial park in 1925, there would have been many remnants of the battle here, including old duckboards, helmets, a fair amount of unexploded ordnance, and even abandoned rifles. Now, with the visitor centre built in the style of a Newfoundland cabin, the soft undulation of trenches and shell-holes grassed over, and areas of the old battlefield cordoned off by fencing, it has become a safe place with its neat paths and signposts. It is now a memorial park rather than a fragment of a battlefield, but still manages to convey an overpowering sense of what happened here. Of the 721 men of the Newfoundland Regiment committed to battle on the 1st July 1916, 619 were either killed or wounded here.

Next page: **TRENCHES AND SHELL HOLES**

This view from the air provides a strange and compelling pattern, and all the more extraordinary because this is just a small piece of the real picture that stretches way beyond the 84 acres purchased by the Government of Newfoundland. Much of the rich Somme farmland that surrounds this Memorial Park has since been turned many times by the plough, but here the old battlefield can still be seen. In the foreground, looking out across the trench lines, is one of the five Caribou memorials to the Newfoundland Regiment placed along the Western Front after the war.

51ST HIGHLAND DIVISION MEMORIAL

Here stands a Highlander in bronze, larger than life, mounted on a platform of Aberdeen granite, placed across the old German front line, and looking defiantly eastwards, as if towards Berlin. The memorial was unveiled in 1924 by Maréchal Foch, and the text of a two-verse poem published in the official programme for the day now appears on a bronze tablet at the entrance to the Memorial Park. The first few lines say it all:

"Tread softly here! Go reverently and slow!
Yea, let your soul go down upon its knees,
and, with bowed head and heart abased, strive hard
to grasp the future gain in this sore loss!
For not one foot of this dark sod but drank
its surfeit of the blood of gallant men,
who, for their faith, their hope, – for Life and Liberty
Here made the sacrifice, – here gave their lives,
And gave right willingly for you and me"

John Oxenham

Right: Y RAVINE

The 'Y' Ravine is a natural feature, a forked gully that probably makes little topographical sense when viewed from ground level, particularly now that it has been fenced off and is firmly out-of-bounds. But from the air something of its value to the Germans can be appreciated. It sits just behind their front line, forming a convenient strongpoint that leads back to the village of Beaumont Hamel. John Masefield described it after the battle as 'one vast hiding place', with galleries and rooms dug deep into the chalk below the high banks, a type of 'gully barracks' in which large numbers of Germans were billeted in relative safety and comfort. But in the final throes of the Somme battle in November 1916, both the 'Y' Ravine and the village were captured by the 51st (Highland) Division. They had fought across the Newfoundlanders' battlefield, and following their impressive victory, the Highlanders were confronted with the grim task of burying the remains of those killed in that earlier battle.

THE ULSTER TOWER WITH MILL ROAD CEMETERY
In the snow.

THE 36TH (ULSTER) DIVISION

The Ulstermen of the 36 (Ulster) Division achieved a remarkable feat of arms on the first day of the Battle of the Somme by advancing further than any other troops in this sector of the line. Moving with great speed and determination, they managed to break through the German front line and capture the Schwaben Redoubt, a stronghold of gun emplacements, trenches and tunnels. In less than three hours of fighting, they reached the German second line trenches, but by then were already dangerously ahead of themselves. They had advanced well ahead of the flanking units on either side, and the Ulstermen were so far forward that they came under fire from British artillery. By nightfall, they had become exposed on all sides and now with dwindling ammunition and other supplies, were driven back by a German counter-attack.

The Ulstermen were certainly gripped by a fervour on that day. Indeed, it has been said that had the advance elsewhere been matched by the performance of the Ulster Division, the outcome on 1st July 1916 might have been very different. A correspondent from The Times watched them '… beginning at a slow walk over No Man's Land and suddenly let loose as they charged over the two front lines of the enemy's trenches shouting "No Surrender, boys".' Four Victoria Crosses were awarded for bravery on that day, and the Division suffered some 5,000 casualties.

The Unionist and Protestant community in Northern Ireland has placed great symbolism on the endeavours of the Ulster Division on the first day of the Somme battle. The Ulster Memorial Tower, built near the site of the Schwaben Redoubt and unveiled in November 1921, emphasizes this symbolism by being different to almost any other memorial in France or Flanders. It was not designed to blend with the surrounding landscape, but is something that would be a reminder of home. The tower is a replica of Helen's Tower at Clandeboye, County Down, where the Ulster Division had trained. Now it stands overlooking the battlefield and not far from the graves of the Ulstermen who died here during the Battle of the Somme.

Left: ## MILL ROAD CEMETERY
Seen at dawn from the edge of Thiepval Wood.

THIEPVAL MEMORIAL FROM THE AIR

The Thiepval Memorial to the Missing of the Somme looks impressive from the air, but it also dominates the surrounding landscape and can be seen from across the battlefield. Designed by Sir Edwin Lutyens and inaugurated in 1932, the memorial bears the names of over 72,000 men who were lost in the Somme battles between July 1915 and March 1918 and for whom there is no known grave. As the years have gone by, and as the remains of soldiers killed on the Somme have been discovered, exhumed and sometimes identified, a name has been quietly removed from the Portland stone tablets on the memorial. The occasional and seemingly inexplicable gap in the long list says it all, and a soldier finally receives the burial he deserves, and with his own gravestone.

Next page: MASH VALLEY

A view directly across No Man's Land towards Ovillers Cemetery showing the open and exposed terrain that the British infantry of the 34th and 8th Divisions crossed on the morning of 1st July 1916.

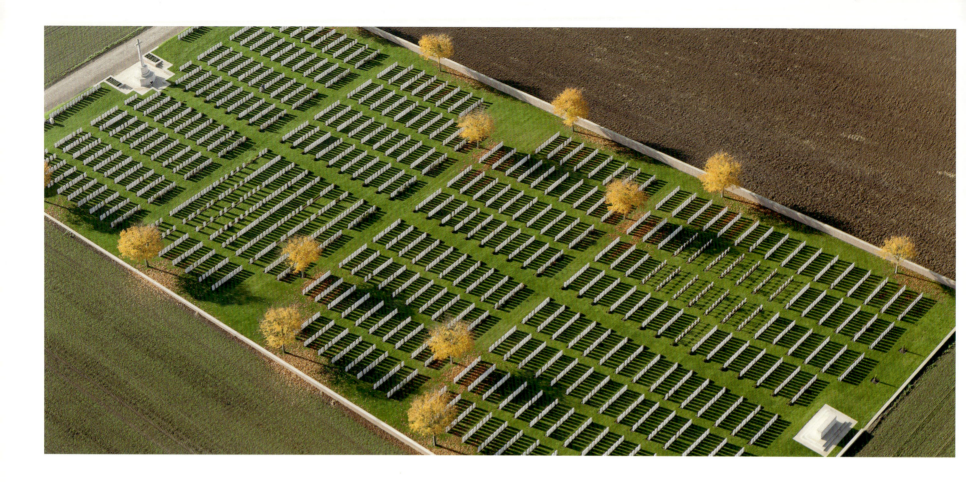

Ovillers Cemetery

The Ovillers Cemetery is in the centre of No Man's Land, looking across the wide and open Mash Valley. This is a huge cemetery by the standards of many others on the Somme, with 3,436 British and 120 French graves, of which many are unidentified. It has a military symmetry in its size and shape, which is poignant since the soldiers buried here, many of whom are not known, were brought from many parts of the battlefield when their bodies were exhumed after the war.

Lochnagar Crater from the air

This almost perfectly formed feature, which no longer looks like a crater and more like something carefully sculpted from the ground, was the result of a massive explosion at 7:28am on the morning of 1st July 1916. Some 60,000 lbs of ammonal had been laid here by the British tunnellers deep below a German position known as the Schwaben Höhe. A Royal Flying Corps pilot, Cecil Lewis, flying nearby, later described what he saw:

'At Boisselle the earth heaved and flashed, a tremendous and magnificent column rose up in the sky. There was an ear-splitting roar drowning all the guns, flinging the machine sideways in the repercussing air. The earth column rose higher and higher to almost 4,000 feet. There it hung, or seemed to hang, for a moment in the air, like the silhouette of some great cypress tree, then fell away in a widening cone of dust and debris'.

Lochnagar Crater was named after a nearby communication trench, and would by now have disappeared had not an Englishman, Richard Dunning, purchased the land from the local farmer and preserved the place as a memorial to those who died here. For this reason, it is now distinct from the surrounding landscape, accompanied by an eerie shadow across the fields-where the trenches once were. Lochnagar has become one of the most visited places along the Western Front, is maintained by a group of volunteers, the Friends of Lochnagar, and is entirely dependent on charitable donations. Richard Dunning describes the crater as an 'open wound on the battlefield', and although its appearance has mellowed over the last century, it retains an immensely powerful presence on the landscape. Fortunately, the dedication of those who care for this place has ensured that it will be here in perpetuity, just like the many memorials and cemeteries that lie nearby.

> *"Through which their bodies grope the*
> *mazy charnel way... seek to distinguish*
> *men from walking trees ..."*
>
> *David Jones*

MAMETZ WOOD FROM THE WELSH MEMORIAL

Both Robert Graves and Siegfried Sassoon fought here with the Royal Welch Fusiliers, and David Jones's long poem 'In Parenthesis' is based in part on his experiences fighting in Mametz Wood. The 38th (Welsh) Division Red Dragon Memorial was unveiled in 1987.

MAMETZ WOOD

The village of Mametz was captured by the British on 1st July 1916 but for further progress to be made on that sector, the large wood that lay beyond needed to be cleared of enemy. There might have been a chance of capturing Mametz Wood early in the battle, but by the time the 38th (Welsh) Division was given the task, the place had become a stronghold occupied by the Prussian Guard. This mismatch in experience could not have been more stark, since the Welshmen were citizen soldiers of Kitchener's New Army, and this was to be their first battle, a baptism of fire.

The wood is thicker and more mature than in 1916, but its irregular shape covering some 220 acres has changed little. Inside the wood prior to the battle the ground was thick with broken undergrowth and wide girthed oak trees together with beech and ash, barbed wire and support trenches. In front of the wood was the German front line trench snaking across the landscape, with a second line of defences on the north-eastern side. It was altogether a formidable obstacle, on a landscape that was deceptive to the eye, standing on a spur of ground with shallow valleys on both sides. Siegfried Sassoon, occupying a German trench in front of Mametz Wood prior to the final attack described it as 'a menacing wall of gloom'. Capturing a trench was just the beginning, since the wood itself needed to be cleared of enemy, and fighting among trees compounds all the obvious factors of war and adds a few more for good measure. Sassoon pitied the Welshmen who were to finish the job in that dark place beyond. 'Our own occupation' he said 'was only a prelude to the pandemonium which converted the green thickets of Mametz Wood to a desolation of skeleton trees and blackened bodies'.

The attack began on 7th July, but with only one brigade of the division committed, and in the face of intensive machine-gun fire, the attempt to take the wood failed. Two days later, the divisional commander, Major-General Ivor Philipps, was relieved of his command, a new and more experienced commander was appointed with orders to take the wood. The 38th (Welsh) Division attacked again on 10th July, and two days later Mametz Wood was finally overrun. It had been a particularly gruelling battle in which the Welshmen had taken nearly 4,000 casualties. Although others fought at Mametz, it has become a place forever associated with Wales and the Welshmen who fought here in July 1916.

The canopy of trees is now dense and thick, and inside the wood many of the undulations and shell-holes of the war remain. It is an atmospheric and timeless place, so much so that one could easily imagine a lone soldier in the wood, a survivor of the battle who has lost his unit, brewing up with his mess tin over a small fire of dried sticks.

Left: CRUCIFIX CORNER

There are many Crucifix Corners in France, but this one is particularly special since the cross here, just south of High Wood, is the original, a little rusty now and bearing a few scars of war. Since it marked a crossroads and was a natural thoroughfare for troops making their way to the front, the area here was frequently shelled by the Germans. It has a simple poignancy since it would have been seen by many soldiers who passed this way, never to return.

THISTLE DUMP CEMETERY

This is the open ground leading up to High Wood, where the 7th Dragoon Guards and Indian 20th Deccan Horse charged forward. For a cavalryman, this open countryside would have seemed an enticing place had it not been for the German machine-guns that were responsible for such heavy casualties here. Despite the enduring hope for a great breakthrough, this was to be the last place during the Somme battle that the cavalry were used in the front line.

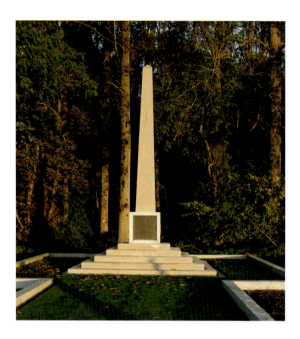

18TH EASTERN DIVISION MEMORIAL

This memorial commemorates the successful attack of the 18th Division on 1st July 1916. This New Army Division was commanded by Major-General Ivor Maxse, aged 54, who had fought at the Battle of Omdurman in 1898. Drawing on his colonial experience, he encouraged junior officers and non-commissioned officers to use their initiative rather than rely on rigid orders. His approach, which demanded detailed planning and rehearsals, later became known as 'battle drill', a term still used today.

MALTKORN FARM CALVARY AND TRONES WOOD

The Calvary is on the site of a farm destroyed during the first month of the Somme battle. Trônes Wood beyond was not an objective on 1st July 1916 but might have been captured that day relatively easily had the battle been more successful elsewhere. It took six days of fighting and some 4000 British casualties before it was finally taken on 14th July. The British Official History describes the topography; 'The wood itself presented an immense obstacle, for its undergrowth, which had not been cut for two years, formed dense thickets, and there was a chaotic tangle of trees and branches brought down by the bombardment. German communication trenches, and a few clearings through which ran light-railway tracks, formed the only easy lines of passage; it was all but impossible to keep direction without a compass bearing.'

DELVILLE WOOD

Delville Wood will be forever associated with South Africa and, as a battle honour, the wood itself is rightly credited to the South Africans who fought here and were largely responsible for its capture. The South African Brigade went into battle for the first time here on 14th July with over 3,153 men but by 20th July only 778 answered the roll call.

The wood is now a tranquil place to walk and wander, with wide rides between the trees named after the streets of London, Edinburgh and Glasgow. The planting is generously spaced, and on a sunny day shafts of light shine through, giving it a bright and airy feel. The passage of time and some gentle landscaping have transformed Delville Wood, and even the shallow and grassed undulations seem entirely natural. Quite a contrast to July 1917, just one year on from the battle fought here:

'Delville Wood still remains terrible. While all the country round is clothed in green, Nature herself seems to have shrunk back shuddering from the Devil's Wood, as if here was a place too awful even for her to attempt to transform. Here and there from the roots of the blasted trees new shoots have sprung and made footstools of leafage against the bare ground, but elsewhere in the wood – and here alone on all these battlefields of last summer, the earth remains brown and barren, with only sparse shreds of grass sprouting reluctantly among the ridge and furrow of the shell-holes'. The Times, 18th July 1917.

The Delville Wood Commemorative Museum, built in 1987, is an impressive building, built in the style of a Vauban fort, but strangely alien to its surroundings. It's a bastion in a foreign land, telling a story of national pride and achievement that goes well beyond its immediate surroundings.

"*At that time, before the battle of the Somme, which opened a new chapter in the history of the war, the struggle had not taken on that grim and mathematical aspect which cast over its landscapes a deeper and deeper gloom.*"

Ernst Jünger, *Storm of Steel*

FRICOURT

17,027 German soldiers lie in this cemetery, of whom 5,057 are in individual graves and 11,970 in massed graves, the Gemeinschaftsgräber. Unlike many of the British cemeteries, this one was not created until the 1920s, when the soldiers buried here were brought in by the French authorities from many parts of the Somme. Sadly, there are many more Germans buried in unmarked graves elsewhere on the battlefield.

MANSEL COPSE

This wood tells a sad and poignant story, and it is all there in the landscape. It was from Mansel Copse that the Devonshire Regiment began their advance on the morning of 1st July 1916, and it was here that a prediction by one of the officers in command was to be tragically proved true. Captain Duncan Lenox Martin had been concerned about a German machine-gun post at the corner of a village cemetery and close to the British front line because its trajectory was straight across the Devons' planned line of advance. He built a plasticine model of the surrounding terrain and it was displayed at the nearby headquarters. But the view from more senior officers was that this and all the other machine-gun posts would be destroyed by the artillery bombardment before the whistle was blown at 7.30 am on 1st July. The soldiers had little to fear.

But the machine-gun post, some 400 yards from the British trenches, had not been destroyed, and many soldiers of the Devons, including Captain Martin, were killed here in the first few minutes of the attack. Another young officer in the same regiment, Lieutenant William Noel Hodgson, had written a poem a few days earlier which, in the final verse, reveals another prediction: his own imminent death.

Both these two officers lie in the cemetery at Mansel Copse, alongside 161 soldiers of the Devonshire Regiment who died that day and two artillerymen who died later. They were buried in their own front line trench, the place that had provided some protection prior to the battle. Very little explanation or understanding is required to grasp what happened here. The front line of the trench can still be seen beyond the neat retaining wall of the cemetery, and in the near distance the corner of the cemetery on the outskirts of Mametz can be discerned. It is all there, as are the words, now in stone, that were placed here on a wooden cross when these soldiers were buried in July 1916.

"The Devonshires Held this trench, The Devonshires Hold it Still"

"By all the glories of the day
And the cool evening's benison
By that last sunset touch that lay
Upon the hills when day was done,
By beauty lavishly outpoured
And blessings carelessly received,
By all the days that I have lived
Make me a soldier, Lord.

By all of all man's hopes and fears
And all the wonders poets sing,
The laughter of unclouded years,
And every sad and lovely thing;
By the romantic ages stored
With high endeavour that was his,
By all his mad catastrophes
Make me a man, O Lord.

I, that on my familiar hill
Saw with uncomprehending eyes
A hundred of thy sunsets spill
Their fresh and sanguine sacrifice,
Ere the sun swings his noonday sword
Must say good-bye to all of this; -
By all delights that I shall miss,
Help me to die, O Lord."

William Noel Hodgson

CAMBRAI

Tanks were seen for the first time on the Somme battlefield in September 1916, but it was at Cambrai, in November 1917, that they appeared en masse. The idea of combining a vehicle with both protection and firepower was not a new one, but the imperative to break the stalemate of trench warfare provided the real catalyst in 1915 that led to the development of the first landship, or 'tank', as it was named to obscure its real purpose. The early tanks were cumbersome and unreliable, and by 1917 certainly had their detractors, but Field Marshal Sir Douglas Haig was now prepared to sanction their large scale use at Cambrai in an attempt to achieve the elusive breakthrough.

The battle began at dawn on 20th November, not with a long and predictable artillery barrage, but with a sudden and intensive burst of over 1,000 guns, the laying of a smoke-screen and a creeping barrage. Then some 300 tanks began to advance slowly across No Man's Land, providing protection to the infantry following closely behind. There were to be some remarkable early successes that day, as the British advanced some 5 miles and assaulted the heavily fortified Hindenburg Line. Back home, the church bells rang for the first time since 1914 and there was a sense that a great battle, perhaps the greatest battle of the war, was about to be won.

But sadly, these early successes could not be maintained. While the British appeared to be making progress, the Germans were preparing their counter-attack, and on 30th November, with the

THE VIEW FROM FLESQUIÈRES RIDGE
TOWARDS BOIS D'HAVRINCOURT.
It was in these woods between Havrincourt and the nearby village of Trescault that the British tanks harboured before the assault.

British now over-extended and many of the tanks knocked out or no longer serviceable, they struck. Most of the gains of the past ten days were recaptured by the Germans, and the British now had to fight to hold their own trenches. The offensive was abandoned and Haig pulled back to consolidate the front line. Some of the bitterest fighting in the last few days of the battle had been around Bourlon Wood, a vast and dense forest that stands on the high ground to the west of Cambrai. Despite repeated efforts to capture the wood, it remained in German hands, as did the town beyond, until nearly the end of the war.

Losses during the Battle of Cambrai were heavy on both sides and broadly equal; the British lost over 44,000, while the Germans losses were probably slightly more. The tank had not delivered the hoped-for victory but it had proved its potential. With further designs and refinements, together with improvements in reliability, it was to play a major role in the battles of 1918.

Tank Deborah

Hidden away, in a barn on the outskirts of the village of Flesquières, is Deborah D51, a Mark IV female tank that was put out of action by a German field gun somewhere in the village on 20th November 1917, the first day of the Cambrai battle. Four members of Deborah's crew were killed in the action, and are buried in a nearby cemetery. Deborah was later buried to become part of an underground shelter, and there she lay until 1998 when she was discovered following an extensive search led by Philippe Gorczynski, a historian of the Battle of Cambrai. Deborah was then raised from the earth and moved to her present resting place, where she now sits quietly, slightly on one side, badly bruised but still somehow magnificent. Her jagged and twisted edges can easily be hidden, like a wounded soldier who turns his disfigured profile away from the camera. On Deborah's 'good side' the symmetry and robustness of the design and structure are still there; lines of neat rivets holding her plates together a century on.
In a symbolic act of remembrance, Deborah will be re-buried close by the cemetery, and her crew, in a ceremony due to take place in November 2017, the 100th anniversary of the battle.

62ND (WEST RIDING) DIVISIONAL MEMORIAL

On the edge of Havrincourt stands the memorial to the 62nd (West Riding) Division, a Territorial formation that fought here in November 1917 and again in March 1918.

FLESQUIÈRES RIDGE SEEN FROM THE SOUTH

This was the rolling landscape that the tanks crossed to break through the Hindenburg line on their way to Flesquières Ridge.

THE AISNE

THE CHEMIN DES DAMES

Named after two of Louis XV's daughters, this is where Napoleon defeated Marshal Blücher in 1814 and where several battles took place during the First World War. An impressive obstacle on the high ground above the Aisne River, the Chemin des Dames proved to be the perfect place for the Germans to halt and turn towards the Allies in September 1914 following the Battle of the Marne. For the British infantry, it had been a particularly tiring and confusing few weeks; first, a rather ragged retreat with some skirmishes and clashes along the way; then a sudden change of direction as the Germans pulled back and the Allies began a pursuit. Both sides were now exhausted, and the reality was that neither had the energy to force a decisive result. Although the Schlieffen Plan had failed and France had not been defeated, the Germans still held an advantage, since they could seek their own place to defend while regaining their strength for later battles.

The BEF on the left and the French on the right crossed the Aisne on the night of 13th September, expecting to push on in pursuit of the Germans the following morning. But this was a place where all the advantages lay with the defender, since it could be held indefinitely. As dawn broke on the morning of 14th September, it was soon clear that the Allies could no longer advance in the open, in the face of machine-gun fire and artillery.

VALLÉE DE FOULON

This rolling rural scene is misleading, particularly when the sun catches the trees and shines across the fields. Behind the photographer is the Chemin des Dames, seized by the Germans in September 1914, and 15 metres below ground is a 16th century limestone quarry first occupied by the French and then captured by the Germans in late January 1915. They named it the Drachenhöhle (Dragon's Cavern), because the weapons placed at each of its seven entrances were there to breathe fire like a seven-headed dragon. The Germans made it comfortable, with electricity and water supply, a place where soldiers could eat, sleep, and pray in almost complete safety; there was even a cemetery down there. Above ground is the Vallée de Foulon where the Nivelle Offensive began in April 1917. Soldiers fought on these fields for much of the next two months, time and again trying to make it to the high ground. Eventually, in late June 1917, the French captured the cavern, but soon the Germans were back, and there was a period when they and the French occupied either ends of the cavern, separated by a hastily built wall. Then the Germans withdrew, but were back in May 1918, holding the cavern until nearly the end of the war.

The soldiers on both sides assumed that this entrenchment would be no more than a welcome halt until mobile warfare recommenced, leading to some form of decisive result. But circumstances had changed, and the shallow shell scrapes dug in the soft ground soon became deeper and later continuous as the Western Front gradually took shape along 450 miles from the sea to the mountains. Both the Allies and the Germans were now faced with an entirely new kind of warfare. Tactics and equipment would evolve as soldiers became familiar with the topography of their sector. Detailed maps were drawn, showing the trench systems as almost permanent features on the ground. For the British and their English-speaking allies, local names would be anglicised, features such as woods and copses would be renamed, and trenches given familiar street names from back home. A war that had begun a month earlier with frenetic movement on all fronts and frontiers had now taken on an entirely different shape and form, a phenomenon on such a scale that it has become unique in the history of warfare. The conflict had become static, and it is for this reason that so many traces of the First World War still exist on the landscape.

The Western Front's topography changes on its journey from the low country of Belgium to the mountains of the Swiss border. There are places where it was better not to fight at all, and sometimes that lesson was learned by both sides. There were other stretches of front line that changed hands frequently and remained contested throughout the war. The Chemin des Dames was a place where most of the advantages favoured the German defender. It had enjoyed a reasonably quiet period for the first two years of the war, until the French decided to attack.

When the fighting came, it was on a massive scale, beginning on 16th April 1917, with the French attacking the Chemin des Dames as part of the Nivelle offensive planned by Général Robert Nivelle. His aim was to seize the German front line before advancing on Laon to the north. But the enemy still held all the advantages, well protected below ground during the preliminary artillery bombardment. The French infantry managed to reach the plateau above the Aisne, but by the time the fighting ended they had suffered some 271,000 casualties. Although the Chemin des Dames and some 20,000 German prisoners had been captured, the Nivelle offensive had been a strategic failure, another disaster in the wake of the huge losses at Verdun the previous year. Morale collapsed, soldiers mutinied, Nivelle was forced to resign, and Général Philippe Pétain was appointed in his place. The British took over the western end of the Chemin des Dames in support of the French and, in October 1917, following the Allied victory at Malmaison, the Germans finally withdrew further north. Then, during the spring of 1918, they were back for their last big offensive, with more fighting along the Chemin des Dames during the closing months of the war.

"Adieu la vie, adieu l'amour,
Adieu toutes les femmes,
C'est bien fini, c'est pour toujours
De cette guerre infâme.
C'est à Craonne sur le plateau
Qu'on doit laisser sa peau
Car nous sommes tous condamnés.
C'est nous les sacrifiés"

La Chanson de Craonne

"Good-bye to life, good-bye to love,
Good-bye to all the women,
It's all over now, we've had it for good
With this awful war.
It's in Craonne up on the plateau
That we're leaving our skins
'Cause we've all been sentenced to die.
We're the ones that they're sacrificing"

Song of Craonne

CRAONNE

Remains of the old cemetery and church at Craonne, a 'Village Détruit' – destroyed by artillery in 1917 and never rebuilt. The village gave its name to a famous song inspired by the mutinies in the French Army following the failure of the Nivelle Offensive in 1917.

141

MEMORIAL TO LOUIS ASTOUL

Sous Lieutenant Louis Astoul, of the 70 ième Sénégalais Bataillon, was killed somewhere near here on the top of the Chemins des Dames during the attack on 16th April 1917; his body was never found. This plateau was a vast open killing ground, ideal for the defender and ghastly for the attacker. Now heavily cultivated, it looked very different in 1917.

REMAINS OF THE FORT DE LA MALMAISON

The Fort de la Malmaison, high on the Chemin des Dames, dates back to the years after the Franco-Prussian War of 1870–71, when the French built a network of forts to protect the north-eastern approaches to Paris. Before the outbreak of war in 1914, the fort had been de-commissioned and sold to a local contractor for demolition. The Germans captured the Chemin des Dames in September 1914, and the remains of the fort, particularly its subterranean galleries, were pressed back into service. The French attempted to recapture the Chemin des Dames during the Nivelle Offensive in April 1917, but the fighting ended in bitter failure, huge casualties, and much recrimination. The Germans not only dominated the high ground with its commanding views across the Aisne Valley, they also used the network of old underground quarries below the ridge where soldiers could shelter from harm's way. In October 1917, the French finally took control of the Chemin des Dames and the tunnels and quarries below ground, following the German withdrawal to the north. But the Germans returned in 1918, and there was more fighting here in the closing months of the war.

Confrécourt, the Aisne Valley

These medieval limestone quarries, now hidden in the forest and close to the old French front line, were occupied by the French Army at the beginning of the war. They were well equipped with living quarters, a hospital with capacity for 400 wounded, and a quartermaster's store for food and ammunition. Set behind, the small, bijou style, officers' quarters, are still there, each with their own fireplace, close to the remains of a narrow gauge railway built to supply the front line. Behind, the ground drops dramatically into a gorge, now overgrown with trees and undergrowth. Like all First World War front lines that have survived, this place would have looked bare and exposed a century ago; thankfully it is now hidden away and protected.

The caves have no information boards or electric lighting inside or, indeed, anything to identify their location until one is there at the front door. Inside, the soldiers left their mark, with carvings on this soft limestone which are both remarkable and poignant. The local landowner, whose family have owned these caves for many years, has gone to great lengths to protect the carvings that could so easily be damaged by vandals or careless visitors. The caves are kept firmly locked, but are opened to visitors by the local history association in the summer months.

Caves at Confrécourt

In the old quarries at Confrécourt, carved in the limestone, are regimental cyphers, badges and rolls of honour, left here by the French units that sheltered in the caves. The quality is remarkable, and many hours must have been spent here by the soldier-craftsmen, gently scratching away under the light of a flickering candle or lamp. On one wall, close to the entrance, is a relief carving of Marianne, the symbol of Liberty of the French Republic. On a bright day, beams of light from the sun seek her out, illuminating the carving in a warm glow on the limestone.

Above: THE CARVED ALTAR IN THE CARRIÈRE
CHAPEAUMONT NEAR BERNY-RIVIERE
*The badges of the regiments who occupied the caves are carved into the
limestone on either side of the altar.*

CHAPELS IN THE CAVES AT CONFRÉCOURT

*Many soldiers pray before battle, even those who have no faith or religion. Here are
two examples of chapels that have been carved deep inside medieval limestone
quarries, impressive examples of soldiers' art. The Chapel of Père Doncoeur (left) is
particularly poignant, as the stairs on the right of the altar, cut into the limestone,
lead directly from the safety of the chapel and the cave, to the front line. For many
soldiers, it was a one-way journey.*

Left: DEATH AT VINGRE

The plaque on the right of this picture honours the bravery of the 298th Infantry Regiment, awarded the Légion d'Honneur in 1914. But on 27th November of that year 19th Company failed to hold its position in the face of the German attack near Vingré. 24 soldiers were accused of desertion, claiming they were following the orders of their officer, who denied all knowledge. Général de Villaret, at Corps Headquarters, ordered that these soldiers were to be tried by a Special Court Martial. At 3pm on 3rd December 1914, judges and prosecutors were appointed, and the defending officer, Lieutenant Bodé, arrived from the front line, knowing nothing of the case, to interview the soldiers. The trial began at 5pm with the regimental commander presiding, and by 7:30pm all 24 soldiers had been found guilty. Six men, Soldats Floch, Gay, Pettelet, Quinault, Durantet and Blanchard, were selected by lot to be executed, 'pour aider les combattants à retrouver le goût de l'obéissance'. (to help the combatants rediscover their taste for obedience). They spent their last night in an old wine cellar (right), and at dawn on 4th December were shot by firing squad with soldiers of their regiment ordered to watch. The Vingré Martyrs were pardoned in 1921, and they are now honoured on the edge of this small village, next to the old wine cellar. Pictures of all six are shown along with the sad but defiant letters they wrote to their loved ones on that last night.

Right: THE CELLAR

This shows where the soldiers spent their last night before execution in the field beyond the memorial.

CHAMPAGNE & ARGONNE

Much of Champagne is agricultural, not particularly prosperous, and off the tourist route. The exception is Reims, with Champagne houses and vineyards on the chalky hills to the south-west and around Epernay. Forty miles to the east, and rising suddenly from the open fields, is the Forêt d'Argonne, 123,000 acres of hilly, rocky, and uneven woodland, where there was much fighting, particularly in the closing few days of the war.

In September 1914, Reims was briefly occupied by the Germans before they were pushed back. Thereafter, the town was frequently shelled, and by 1918 much of it lay in ruins. On 10th December 1914, in an attempt to end the war quickly, Joffre launched an offensive concentrating on the area between Reims and Verdun. While the French were stronger in numbers, it was the Germans who had the advantages: good trenches and machine-guns that could dominate the open ground. Somehow the French hung on until mid-March, despite appalling weather, huge casualties, and no real gains. An even larger offensive in September 1915 also ended in failure.

1916 was quieter as the French were drawn towards Verdun, just as the Germans had intended. On 17th April 1917, attacks took place east of Reims and along the Chemin des Dames, as part of the Nivelle Offensive. The battle lasted over a month, and while there were a few minor gains, these small successes, all at a huge cost, had no real bearing on the outcome of this ghastly battle. 1917 had been a dire year, with a substantial corner of France remaining firmly in German hands.

In the early hours of 21st March 1918, General Erich Ludendorff launched the Kaiserschlacht (Emperor's Battle), his last great throw of the dice in which he intended to drive a wedge between the Allies and win the war. The Germans had a numerical advantage if they struck swiftly before the Americans arrived, and their new stormtrooper tactics were ideally suited to the advance. The battle began along the Hindenburg Line close to St. Quentin, and within a few days they had swept across the old Somme battlefield with the Germans close to Amiens, opening up a 50 mile gap in the Allied lines. But then they faltered, through a combination of fatigue and ill-discipline while the Allies, badly shaken, remained steady.

Further German offensives followed with limited success. Then, on 15th July 1918, came their final attempt, Friedensturm (Peace Offensive), with attacks on either side of Reims. The Germans managed to cross the Meuse, forming a salient, but the Allies were now into their war-winning stride. The French and British had grasped the lessons, and this battle marked the first really successful French counter-attack of the war. All-arms cooperation was working, and the Allied air forces were playing a key role. The Americans were learning fast, and keen to make their mark, whatever the cost.

This final German offensive in Champagne was a turning point for the Allies, although the cost had been huge; some 130,000 Allied and 200,000 German casualties in this battle alone. For the Germans, it was a culminating point. Four months on, the offensive, with over 1 million casualties, and some 29,300 soldiers captured, their morale now disintegrating. Despite their losses, the Allies were getting stronger with 300,000 American soldiers arriving every month. For the first time in the war, with only weeks left before victory, the outcome could be predicted with confidence. The last phase had begun.

Right: WIRE AT MASSIGES

La Main De Massiges

These recently excavated trenches, both French and German, have a raw and authentic feel to them. In September 1914, following the Battle of the Marne, the Germans pulled back, halted and dug in along a line running from the sea to the mountains, choosing the high ground from which to defend their territorial gains. The Allies closed up on this new front line, and in places No Man's Land was a matter of a few yards wide. So it was here at La Main de Massiges, where the topsoil has now been removed to reveal the chalk subsoil, the shell-holes, trenches, and all the rusty metal detritus of war. Although not easily discernible from ground level, the clue to this place is in the name 'The Hand of Massiges' since the front line trenches that follow the ridges and spurs that flow across this wide landscape resemble the shape of a hand. These trenches and the tunnels beneath were fought over many times during the war. As the years go by, this place will gradually become more 'curated' and there are already a few information boards, as well as old photographs which uncannily depict almost the same scene as today. But in all other respects the place remains open, with no signposting, visitor centre, or facilities of any kind. The car park is a field at the end of a rough track, and artefacts lie where they were found, hopefully where they will stay. A little way behind the trenches are the remains of a narrow-gauge railway, command posts, and quartermaster stores. If there is anywhere on the Western Front where one might expect to see a French soldier, dressed in his fighting order, emerge from his billet ready for duty in the trenches, it is here.

Next page: FRENCH TRENCHES

153

FERME DE NAVARIN

Just south of the village of Sommepy-Tahure is the Monument Aux Morts des Armées de Champagne at Ferme de Navarin, both a monument and an ossuary in which the bones of some 10,000 unidentified soldiers lie. The monument stands on the site of Rougemont farm, named after the red soil that now seems to have been buried by the white chalk brought to the surface by the war. Three statues sit on top of this pyramid-shaped monument: In the centre, Général Henri Gouraud, who suggested the monument and unveiled it in 1924; to his right, the sculptor Maxime Réal del Sarte's brother, who died at the Chemin des Dames; and to his left Lieutenant Quentin Roosevelt, the youngest son of President Theodore Roosevelt, shot down in July 1918 while serving as a fighter pilot with the United States Army Air Service. Général Gouraud, commanding the French 4th Army from 1916, was buried alongside his own soldiers in 1946, in the crypt inside the monument. The body of Quentin Roosevelt, buried by the Germans in 1918, was later exhumed and reburied at the American cemetery behind Omaha Beach in Normandy, next to his brother Ted, a brigadier-general who died of a heart attack in July 1944.

Surrounding the monument, and set back from the busy and unbending dual carriageway that speeds the traveller past this miserable place, are the rather forlorn remains of trenches, barbed wire, and shell-holes. It is rather depressing, and all the more so in the knowledge that the cost of the monument was raised by subscriptions, many of them in the form of small donations accompanied by sad letters from the widows and children of those who died here.

BUTTE DE VAUQUOIS

Vauquois was destroyed in February 1915, and only a few fragments and traces of the village on either side of this extraordinary landscape have survived and been preserved. What is here was created not just by shells from above, but by mines from below and, for much of the war, the scene was constantly changing, like a boiling lava. Somehow the destructive energy from both below and above ground has fused together to create a topographical monster which had not really mellowed at all, despite the grass, the paths, and the surrounding trees. It is impossible to visit Vauquois without contemplating the terrible loss of life that took place here.

Above: **GERMAN TRENCHES AT VAUQUOIS**

Just to the east of the Argonne Forest, the trenches provide an extraordinary permanency to the landscape. They were built to last.

THE KRONPRINZ LAIR

On the outbreak of war, Kronprinz Wilhelm of Germany was appointed by his father to command the Fifth Army, although the Kaiser had no illusions about his son's experience or ability to command an entire army. Serving alongside the Crown Prince was Lieutenant-General Konstantin Schmidt von Knobelsdorf, his formidable chief of staff, who, in all but name, was to be the real commander. The Kaiser made this very clear to his son: 'What he tells you, you must do'. In 1916, General Ludendorff gave the task of conducting the Verdun offensive to the Fifth Army, and the photograph on the right is the Crown Prince's Headquarters during that battle. Deep in the woods and some distance from the front line, this place has a 'safely quartered' feel about it, with a stylish ambience that somehow seems to match the rather frivolous nature of the Fifth Army Commander.

ILS N'ONT PAS PASSÉ

AUX MORTS DE LA 69ᵉᵐᵉ DIVISION

SOLDATS - 251ᵉ-254-267-287-306-332-D'INFANTERIE-ARTILLEURS-SAPEURS CAVALIERS

LEURS ADMIRATEURS-LEURS CAMARADES-LEUR CHEF RECONNAISSANT LE GENERAL TAUFFLIEB

VERDUN

With the costly and indecisive battles of 1915 now over, both the Allies and the Germans were desperately looking for ways of breaking the stalemate of trench warfare. Earlier in the year, the British had tried an indirect approach, with their amphibious landings on the Gallipoli peninsula; the campaign lingered on until December, and was a dismal failure. For the French at home, the obsession with the offensive had led them into one tragic battle after another. Now the Germans, who had relied more on holding onto ground than launching attacks, were about to make attrition the centre-piece of their strategy. General Erich von Falkenhayn believed that victory could only be won on the Western Front, and he would find a place 'the retention of which the French Command would be compelled to throw in every man they have'. His aim was simply to 'bleed the France army white' in an operation where killing soldiers was the primary aim.

Falkenhayn chose Verdun with its surrounding forts, sitting in a salient that was vulnerable to attack from two sides. Verdun was an old fortress town dating back to Roman times, and it had great symbolism for France. The Meuse flows through the town, and the countryside beyond is mostly agricultural land, chalk and clay, gently rolling, with a few ridges and many woods and smaller copses. Falkenhayn calculated that the French would hold Verdun at all costs; it was the ideal place, therefore, to inflict casualties.

The German heavy artillery bombardment began at 07:15 on 21st February 1916, and it came as a complete surprise to the French. Some 1,400 guns were placed along an 8 mile front, delivering 100,000 shells an hour onto Verdun and the surrounding area. The German infantry attacked later that day, overrunning many of the French front line trenches. Lieutenant-Colonel Émile Driant, commanding two chasseurs battalions at Bois des Caures, 10 miles north of Verdun, mustered all the infantry he could find, sending them forward into trenches in an attempt to hold the line. Driant led from the front, and was killed early in the battle, aged 60.

On 25th February the Germans seized Fort Douaumont, and did so surprisingly easily. Since this mighty fort was some three miles behind the front line, the French had deemed it to be less important, removing most of its heavy guns and leaving it with only a small garrison of around 100 men. But now that Douaumont had been lost, there was an imperative for its recapture.

The situation was dire, but somehow Joffre remained calm. He dismissed Général Langle de Cary, responsible for the defence of Verdun, and appointed Général Henri Philippe Pétain in his place, making it clear that any commander that gave ground to the Germans would be court-martialled. Pétain promised Joffre that Verdun would not fall: 'Ils ne passeront pas' – 'They

> *"We all carried the smell of dead bodies with us. The bread we ate, the stagnant water we drank... Everything we touched smelled of decomposition due to the fact that the earth surrounding us was packed with dead bodies..."*
>
> *A soldier's letter home*

shall not pass'. Since Falkenhayn was less concerned about capturing Verdun, his aim being the maximum number of French casualties, Pétain's resolve to hold it at all costs proved a virtue for the Germans. Pétain was extremely determined. He had an eye for the details of his defensive plan, he reorganised his artillery, and placed special emphasis on maintaining a good supply route into Verdun, the road which became known as the 'Voie Sacrée', the 'Sacred Road'. Reinforcements and ordnance flowed in to the extent that the road was nose-to-tail with vehicles and often deluged with mud.

Over the next few weeks, the Germans kept up the pressure with more attacks. Intensive fighting took place around the high ground at Le Mort Homme close to the River Meuse, and on 9th April the Germans launched another huge offensive, gradually making progress toward the remaining forts. On 29th May they captured Le Mort Homme and on 7th June Fort Vaux fell. The small garrison there had held out splendidly under Commandant Raynal, who had inflicted over 2,500 casualties on the Germans. The French had fought for a week and the conditions inside had been appalling, to the extent that German soldiers above ground could smell the stench emanating from its shafts. The latrines had been cut off by falling masonry, and the siege only came to an end when the French ran out of water. After Raynal finally surrendered, and in recognition of his gallantry during the siege, he was received by Kronprinz Wilhelm, commanding the German Fifth Army.

By late June the Germans were close to Verdun as they attempted to capture the inner forts of Souville and Tavannes, but their progress was checked by the opening of the Somme offensive on 1st July. This proved a turning point, because from here on the Germans were no longer capable of reinforcing Verdun with more troops.

The French recaptured Fort Douaumont in October and Fort Vaux the following month. The Battle of Verdun finally ended in December, by which time the overall casualties at Verdun had reached at least 800,000, although it is impossible to be more precise. The offensive had lasted longer than any other during the war, the honour of France had been preserved, but at an almost indescribable cost.

The Verdun battlefield is an extraordinary place, and the topography alone, leaving aside the ebb and flow of this long battle, takes time to understand and assimilate. The overall picture is further complicated by the many forts that fold themselves into the landscape and the thick forests and woods that existed before the war, were completely destroyed during the fighting, and are now even more extensive and thicker than ever. Ironically, all the forts have survived in one form or another, while a good number of the villages around Verdun were completely destroyed and never rebuilt. Finally, there are the cemeteries and memorials, quite different in style to other national monuments of the war.

The forts that surround Verdun all predate the First World War since they were mostly built in the decade following the Franco-Prussian War of 1870–71, at a time when France had already lost land to the east and was determined not to lose more.

Right: DOUAUMONT FRENCH NATIONAL CEMETERY AND OSSUARY

During the First World War, many of these forts were rendered redundant and played no real part, while others, particularly Forts Douaumont and Vaux, saw some of the most desperate fighting of the entire war. These two forts are now open to the public, and they still retain a rawness that can send a chill down one's spine. Some of the other forts can be more difficult to find, hidden away in the undergrowth, and not always easily accessible. Vast in their construction, and often only revealing a fraction of themselves, they are like battleships, locked in a dense landscape, entirely reliant on their guns and their exits and entrances. They speak of another era of European history, when frontiers were thick lines, not just on the map, but on the ground as well. Verdun was a chosen route to Paris for the invader, and so this area became a network of forts, with the town in the centre of the huge defensive web.

Woods and forests can be dark and uncomfortable particularly on a winter's afternoon as the light dims and the folds in the ground among the broken branches begin to blur. But around Verdun, there is more to ponder while walking through one of these places. This is where men died in their thousands; their remains are in the soil below, along with the traces of the millions of shells that fell here, some packed with poisonous chemicals. While it may be tempting to wander away from the marked tracks, it is not advisable.

The French fought and died on every sector of the Western Front, and this is not always as obvious on the well-trodden WWI tourist route, since the absence of big memorials and cemeteries does not convey the full story. But Verdun is different, and the symbolism of this place is so overpowering. Verdun has a grimness and intensity that the rolling Somme landscape does not. It became a charnel house where the task in hand was to kill as many of the enemy as possible. The memorials are everywhere, and they express the anguish of loss and bereavement, and on a staggering scale.

FORT DOUAUMONT

Below this extraordinary landscape that looks like another world is Fort Douaumont. The fort was built in the 1880s during the aftermath of the Franco-Prussian War, and is the largest of a network of forts intended to defend Verdun. But when the Belgian forts failed to prevent the German invasion in August 1914, the French decided that this fort and its like had seen their day. Consequentially, the French lost the fort easily to the Germans in February 1916, recapturing it in October, but only after a fearsome battle.

FORTIFICATIONS
AT FORT DOUAUMONT

These rusting metal turrets still look out over the landscape, but without the uninterrupted view that would have existed in 1916, when there were no trees or vegetation anywhere.

170

WASHROOMS

Over the years water has come through the ceilings in the soldiers' washroom, forming stalactites, while on the wash-basins themselves and on the floor, stalagmites have appeared.

GUN EMPLACEMENT

This shows internal workings of Fort Douaumont's 155 mm gun turret below ground. It could be elevated and then retracted for protection. Although the turret has almost certainly seized up or been bent in its smooth cradle, these mechanisms inside the fort still look as if they might even work.

COLONEL DRIANT'S COMMAND POST

Deep in the woods at the Bois des Caures, and not far from the front line, is Lieutenant-Colonel Emile Driant's command post. At 07.15 am on 21st February 1916, the German guns began a bombardment along a 15 mile front and by late afternoon 6 infantry divisions were advancing on a 5 mile frontage. By the following day, the Germans were in the Bois des Caures, where the 61 year old Driant and his two battalions of Chasseurs fought desperately to hold the line. Driant was killed that day, and of 1,200 of his men who fought in the wood, only 100 managed to get out alive.

Driant's command post was badly damaged by artillery during the war and was later preserved as an historic monument. In the years following the war, plaques and memorials were placed here to remember the units and Chasseurs who fought here.

PAMART CASEMENT FOR MACHINE-GUN

Designed to encase two machine-guns, this strange structure looks like a 20th century version of an ancient Egyptian god, breathing fire.

St Mihiel Salient, Tranchee de la Soif (Trench of Thirst)

Here, deep in the Apremont forest, are the remains of trenches gradually melding into the wooded landscape. The small town of St. Mihiel on the River Meuse was seized by the Germans in September 1914 and was to become the most western point of a salient that remained in German hands for most of the war. The French tried hard during 1914 and 1915 to remove the salient, but it was not until September 1918, by which time the Germans were beginning to withdraw, that this was achieved by the Americans in a huge mobile operation.

ALSACE VOSGES

Alsace was occupied by Germany during the Franco-Prussian War of 1870, and when war broke out in August 1914 France immediately crossed the border in an attempt to recover this lost territory. Twice, the French managed to occupy the city of Mulhouse, and on each occasion they were driven back by the Germans. They tried again on 19th August, but again failed. By now, the Western Front was taking shape along the high ground of the Vosges Mountains, a line that was to stay broadly the same for the remainder of the war.

Early in 1915 the French began to launch attacks on the German front line high up in the mountains. As with many other sectors of the Western Front, the French had the disadvantage since the Germans had chosen their defensive positions first, and in the mountains this meant the peaks, sometimes 3,000 feet above sea-level. Critically, the Germans were also able to place their heavy artillery where they could dominate the surrounding countryside, the hillsides and the valleys below. The conditions here were often extreme, particularly in winter, with freezing temperatures and thick snow on the ground.

By the summer of 1915, the Germans had made considerable effort to improve their positions hereto the extent that they were virtually impenetrable. They had cut their trench systems directly into the rock, creating tunnels and underground bunkers, laying barbed wire between the rocks and in the escarpments. A combination of the elevations between the front lines, the trees and bushes, interspersed with rocks and gullies, made these places challenging for both defender and attacker, but the former always had the edge. Although there was much fighting here in the early days, once established, the front lines, in places only a few yards apart, hardly changed for the rest of the war. The Linge ridge in the Vosges was one sector where the French desperately tried to make good their positions before the line firmed up and movement became all but impossible. With their mountain troops, the Chasseurs Alpins, the French attacked along the Linge on 20th July 1915. The battle was to last for three months, and some 10,000 Frenchmen and 7,000 Germans were killed during the offensive. Given the rocky nature of the terrain, both sides relied upon particularly nasty methods such as gas attacks and flamethrowers. But still, there were no significant territorial gains or losses; this front was to change very little until the end of the war in November 1918.

Some of the most intensive fighting in the Vosges took place at Hartmannswillerkopf, also known as the Vieil Armand, a rocky spur 3,000 feet high above the Rhine valley, where some 30,000 soldiers, mostly French, died during the war. There is a French national monument and cemetery here, and around the top of the spur are many examples of both French and German front line trenches. Throughout 1915, the French fought to seize control of this feature, with its commanding view across Alsace. But by the end of that year, wiser heads prevailed, partly because there were greater demands for resources elsewhere. This was a place where it was better to hold ground rather than seek any decisive breakthrough, and so both sides kept the minimum forces here to maintain the status quo. This perhaps explains why these trench systems, with their underground bunkers and interconnecting tunnels, are so impressive. They have a permanency which defies simple logic, but then there is so much about the First World War that, a century on, we find difficult to understand.

MEMORIAL ON THE SUMMIT
The Aussichtsfelsen (The Lookout) unveiled in 1922 to commemorate the deeds of the French 152 ième Régiment d'Infanterie.

Next page: ## FRENCH DEFENCES
A century later nothing much seems to have changed. It is pleasant to walk here on a warm summer's day, but to survive during winter, perched on the side of a mountain, within range of the enemy's heavy guns, would have been very different.

FRENCH & GERMAN TRENCH LINES
There was no natural cover here a century ago, but now the vegetation is gradually reclaiming the mountainside, although these trench lines will never entirely disappear.

LOOKING OUT ACROSS ALSACE

Stand here, looking out across Alsace, and some of the madness
of this place makes sense. The army that holds this high ground
controls the landscape for miles in all directions. For the Germans,
it was a route to the Rhine valley, and had to be held, while, for the
French, it was part of France, and they wanted it back.

THE RETREAT & ADVANCE

OPERATION MICHAEL

The Germans launched Operation Michael at 4:40am on 21st March 1918 with a huge artillery barrage along a frontage of over 50 miles. The attack was not unexpected, and Field Marshal Haig had for some weeks been warning his commanders to be ready for a 'big hostile offensive of prolonged duration'. He was worried particularly about the area around Arras, at the centre of the British front line, and also Ypres, close to the Channel ports. But most of all, he was concerned about the lack of manpower and a reluctance in London to acknowledge the threat along the Western Front.

The British Fifth Army was not ready nor prepared for the attack when it came and, within three days, the Germans had crossed the Somme River in pursuit. The old battlefield was overrun, Albert captured, and Amiens was within the Germans' sights. They had advanced nearly 40 miles, further than any offensive of the war, but then began to falter. The Germans were exhausted, their casualties had been huge, and they had now reached a culminating point, a moral and physical paralysis that came close to defeat, but not quite. Although more German attacks followed, Operation Michael had been a strategic failure that was to precipitate the last phase of the war: an Allied offensive where, for the first time, the landscape was to become the handmaiden of manoeuvre.

The Hundred Days Offensive opened on 18th July 1918, with the French launching a counter-attack that drove the Germans back over the Marne and to the Aisne. On 8th August, the Battle of Amiens began, with Australians and Canadians leading, advanced nine miles that was later described by General Ludendorff as 'The black day of the German Army', a turning point in the war. The issue for the Germans was no longer victory, but survival.

The BEF was now at the top of its game. Its equipment and tactics were better than ever, tanks were now more plentiful, reliable and mobile, and being employed boldly as the spearhead of the advance. The French had retained their determination despite terrible losses, the Americans had arrived and, for the first time in nearly four years, the offensive had become the predominant phase of war. By contrast, the Germans' offensive had been their undoing.

By early September, the Germans were back behind their prepared defences along the Hindenburg Line, but here they steadied and turned again to face their enemy. In the meantime, the Allies had managed to 'pinch out' some of the salients held by the Germans for much of the war. Now, with Maréchal Foch orchestrating Allied attacks along the entire Western Front, and with Americans in the front line and getting stronger by the day, the final die had been cast. The attacks would take place along three lines of advance: in Flanders, with British, French and Belgian troops; in the centre around Cambrai and St. Quentin, with Haig commanding three British armies and one French army; and to the south, in the wooded region of the Meuse and the Argonne, with the French and Americans.

On 27th September, the British attacked the Hindenburg Line on the Canal du Nord, followed two days later by the St. Quentin Canal just beyond. Fighting was fierce and casualties were high, but within a week the line had been broken. It was a similar story along the front, although the Germans continued to fight fiercely in some places and sporadically in others, as they fell back to their own frontier. At the political level, overtures for peace had begun, and when the war ended, at 11am on 11th November 1918, the British Army was back in Mons, where its first battle had been fought, in August 1914.

THE AUSTRALIANS AT VILLERS-BRETONNEUX

Villers-Bretonneux is less than 10 miles from the strategically important city of Amiens, some 40 miles from the coast. Although there were others involved in the battle here, it has rightly become a special place for the Australians, since it was Australian troops that saved Villers-Bretonneux from being captured by the Germans in early April 1918, and it was Australians who recaptured it three weeks later following another more successful German attack. On 8th August, the Australians were again in action here, leading the Allied advance that began the Hundred Days Offensive.

This is an open, flat, and rolling landscape, and the outskirts of Amiens can just be seen in the far distance, to the right of the photograph. The Australian National Memorial not only commemorates the fighting that took place around Villers-Bretonneux in April 1918, but also the names of those many thousands of Australian soldiers who died in France and have no known grave. When the memorial, designed by Sir Edwin Lutyens, was unveiled by King George VI in 1938, it bore nearly 11,000 names. In the intervening years, some of those soldiers have been identified elsewhere and given their own graves, and so the number of missing shown has diminished, but only slightly. On 31st August 1944, soldiers of the Household Cavalry, advancing towards the Somme, briefly stopped at the entrance to the memorial and paid their respects before dropping down into the river valley, to seize the bridge at Corbie, just over two miles to the north.

SECOND BATTLE OF THE MARNE

The battle here began on 15th July 1918, and it was to be the Germans' final attempt at a major offensive. Two days later they had been halted and then, the next day, the Allies launched their massive coordinated attacks along the length of the Western Front. This impressive and powerful sculpture, Les Fantômes, by Paul Landowski, stands on the Butte de Chalmont near Oulchy-le-Château in the Aisne, where the outcome of the Second Battle of the Marne was decided. Within three days of the launching of the Allies' counter-offensive on 18th July, the Germans had been pushed back across the Marne to the Aisne, where they had been for much of the war. But the offensive did not end there. This was a turning point as the Allies continued to advance along the whole Western Front until the war ended on 11th November 1918.

There is no triumphalism in this sculpture. These are the ghosts of seven French servicemen, a recruit, sapper, machine-gunner, grenadier, colonial soldier, an infanteer, and an airman, symbolically raised from the trenches where Landowski had seen them lying dead. They stand with their eyes closed, surrounding and protecting a naked and martyred hero, symbolising the suffering of mankind. Below the sculpture, on the edge of the road, is Marianne, the symbol of France, defiantly holding a shield bearing the figures of Liberté, Egalité and Fraternité.

"Retreat? Hell, we just got here!"

US Marine Captain Lloyd W. Williams at Belleau wood

THE AMERICANS IN THE FIRST WORLD WAR

The United States declared war on Germany on 6th April 1917 and three months later soldiers of the American Expeditionary Force (AEF) began to arrive in France under the command of General John J. Pershing. It began as a small army that had never deployed overseas before, and needed to expand to a much larger fighting force. Pershing's intention was that US forces would serve as part of a single US-led army, but this took time to achieve, given the challenges of preparing for a new type of war. In October 1917, American troops entered the trenches for the first time along a relatively quiet sector, as the steady build-up of troops continued well into 1918.

The Allies had been fighting an attritional and static war for three years when the Americans began arriving on the Western Front. By this time, the British and French had become extremely skilled in the tactics of trench warfare, but they were also weary of war and had lost most of the enthusiasm and vigour of 1914. By contrast, the Americans were eager to press ahead in all respects, while questioning the inevitable caution that had crept into Allied planning. Pershing was keen that the AEF was allocated its own sector of the front line, but equally anxious to conduct a more mobile form of warfare. Perhaps the memory of the sieges of Petersburg and Vicksburg during the US Civil War some 65 years earlier were still in the US Army's collective memory, but Pershing did not have long to wait. The Germans launched their Kaiserschlacht offensive on 21st March 1918, and from then on events unfolded dramatically.

Belleau Wood was the first major battle fought by the Americans on the Western Front, described by General Pershing as the most important battle fought by US forces since the Civil War. It was a baptism of fire, a desperate plugging of a collapsing Allied front line following the seizing of Belleau Wood by the Germans on 1st June 1918. It was the task of two US Army divisions to secure the line, but it was the action of the 4th US Marine Brigade in retaking Belleau Wood that is remembered. Their first challenge was to cross the wheat fields and meadows covered by German machine-guns, and it was here that the Marines took the highest casualties in their history, only surpassed 25 years later, fighting the Japanese in the Pacific. Once inside the wood, the battle gradually turned to the Marines' favour, and it was just as confusing and brutal as the fighting that took place three years earlier when the BEF held up the Germans in the Forêt de Retz, some 15 miles to the north-east. There were other similarities, since this kind of close-quarter battle, fought with bayonet and rifle and amongst trees, was a new experience for both the British and Americans. The difference at Belleau was that it was now the Germans who were retreating, and as a consequence, it is impossible to know how many casualties they took. For the Americans, it was an important and symbolic victory, their first on the European mainland.

BELLEAU WOOD
Rain filled crater and destroyed artillery piece.

MONTSEC

This splendid and imposing memorial commemorates not only the massive US attack into the St. Mihiel Salient in mid-September 1918, but also the Meuse-Argonne offensive in the last few days of the war and the American contribution along other sectors of the Western Front. The St. Mihiel attack was on a massive scale due to Pershing's determination to resist Foch's wishes and not to divide his forces to other tasks. Despite the appalling weather and muddy roads that made resupply more difficult, the Americans made swift progress as they attacked the salient from both the west and the south. Well supported by Allied aircraft and artillery as well as French tanks manned by Americans under the command of Colonel George S. Patton, the advancing infantry soon captured all their objectives. There was to be no German counter-attack, since the enemy were soon withdrawing to the east. Young American commanders had led from the front, and although some aspects of the battle remain controversial, this was another example of US determination and fighting spirit. The memorial at Montsec is impressive and distinctly American in style with its towering colonnades; one could be in Washington DC.

MONTFAUCON

The Meuse-Argonne Offensive, part of the last great Allied push along the Western Front, began on 26th September, and continued until the very end, as Pershing carried on relentlessly to launch attacks onto the Germans. The scale of the offensive was huge, and much of its planning had been overseen by Colonel George C. Marshall, who had also been responsible for planning the St. Mihiel operation and the logistical moves that followed its successful conclusion.

Now that the armies were moving forward, landscape and terrain were to take on an even more important significance than during the days of static trench warfare. The Meuse-Argonne region was thickly overgrown, there were few roads through the forests, and the Germans still had the ability to choose well-defended strongholds from which they could surprise their enemy. Along their sector, the Americans made some impressive advances in the first few days, but a determined German response, further frustrated by logistical challenges, led to a pause in the offensive on 30th September. When the fighting began again four days later, the Germans were better prepared, and the last month of the war became something of an old-style slogging match. Casualties on both sides were huge and evenly matched. On 4th November, a week before the Armistice, the Americans crossed the Meuse. General George S. Patton, as commander of the US Third Army, was to return there in December 1944 when the Germans launched the Ardennes offensive that helped to prolong the Second World War for another five months. But by November 1918, the Germans really were finished.

The photograph above shows the ruined church at Montfaucon d'Argonne. The strange structure on the left, which seems to somehow blend with the much older remains that surround it, is a German observation post.

MEUSE-ARGONNE AMERICAN CEMETERY

All cemeteries are special and hallowed places, but there is something particularly moving about this one, recording the names of the 14,246 American servicemen buried here and 954 missing in action. Soldiers from Iowa, New York, South Carolina, Michigan, Tennessee, Georgia, and many other US states, came a long way to fight here.

AUSTRALIAN 4TH DIVISION MEMORIAL

This memorial, near the village of Bellenglise and above the St. Quentin Canal, is where the war finally ended for the 4th Australian Division in late September 1918. Having successfully broken the Hindenburg Line here, this was the last time that the Division saw action. Not far from a busy dual carriage-way, the memorial stands alone on the open landscape, guarded now by these tall modern sentinels.

MEMORIAL TO THE BRITISH 46TH (NORTH MIDLAND) DIVISION

This modest and rather forlorn looking divisional memorial stands close to the St. Quentin road at Bellenglise. It was this division that took the bridge at Riqueval.

RIQUEVAL BRIDGE ST QUENTIN CANAL

In 1918, the Riqueval Bridge on the St.Quentin Canal was on a major German supply route. It is now on a quiet and unkempt road, and surrounded by trees and undergrowth. Other than that, very little has changed in the last century. The bridge was captured intact on 29th September 1918 by soldiers of the North Staffordshire Regiment before the Germans could detonate their demolition charges.

On the headstones:

1528 GUARDSMAN
HARRY ROBINSON
COLDSTREAM GUARDS
27TH SEPTEMBER 1918 AGE 22

SON OF
CHAS. & MARY ROBINSON
OF OUSEBURN YORK
GOD BE WITH YOU

20810 LANCE CPL.
T. N. JACKSON V.C.
COLDSTREAM GUARDS
27TH SEPTEMBER 1918, AGE 21

"FATHER FORGIVE THEM
FOR THEY KNOW NOT
WHAT THEY DO"
S. LUKE 23.34

20710 GUARDSMAN
J. R. GILLEY
COLDSTREAM GUARDS
27TH SEPTEMBER 1918 AGE 26

SADLY MISSED
AND DEARLY LOVED BY ALL

GRAINCOURT, CANAL DU NORD 1918

On 27th September 1918, the leading platoon of the 1st Battalion Coldstream Guards came under heavy machine-gun fire from a strong post under a destroyed iron bridge and was unable to advance further. Captain Cyril Frisby called for volunteers, rushed forward with three other soldiers, climbed down into the canal, and captured two machine-guns and 12 men, despite being under intense fire. One of the soldiers with him, Lance-Corporal Thomas Jackson, was the first to volunteer. He survived the attack, but later that day was killed when he was the first to jump into a German trench that needed clearing. Both Frisby and Jackson were awarded the Victoria Cross for the same action, a rare feat indeed.

SANDERS KEEP CEMETERY

On the high ground to the south-east of the bridge is this small cemetery that can be seen on the horizon where Lance-Corporal Thomas Jackson VC is buried.

BOURLON WOOD

A view of Bourlon Wood from the south-west. Deceptive in size, the wood is over a mile deep and the scene of bitter fighting at the end of the Battle of Cambrai in late 1917. The wood was captured in October 1918 by the Canadians when they swept through supported by tanks and aircraft during the Hundred Days Offensive. The scene looked very different in 1918; the trees had been mostly shattered and those that remained were stripped bare.

Sucrerie Cemetery, seen in the foreground, is remote, and can only be accessed after a half mile walk across farmland near Graincourt-les-Havrincourt. The area was captured by the 62nd (West Riding) Division on the 20th November 1917, and again, after a hard struggle, by the 63rd (Royal Naval) Division on the 27th September 1918.

St Syphorien Cemetery near Mons

Mons has an extraordinary and enduring symbolism. It is where the first British soldier to die in the war, Private John Parr, was killed on 21st August 1914, and where the last British soldier, Private George Ellison, fell at around 9:30 am on 11th November 1918, just an hour and a half before the Armistice. Perhaps this was a coincidence, or more likely a consequence of the German occupation that had lasted throughout. Either way, it matters not. These two soldiers lie in St Symphorien Military Cemetery, on the outskirts of Mons, and their graves are within sight of each other. In a few short strides, one can easily touch both gravestones. But it is more difficult to begin to contemplate all that happened between the deaths of these two young soldiers. One was killed in the first few weeks of the war; while the other survived almost to the end. Both were tragedies, in equal measure.

Clearing the battlefields of the dead was not easy, and the task of gathering and burying the dead and making the battlefields safe was to continue long after the war. There were miles of barbed wire and pickets, unexploded ordnance, including gas canisters and objects that looked inert but were not. Soldiers' bodies are still being discovered to this day, and the shells, the 'duds' that failed to do their business a century ago are slowly being brought to the surface again.

PRIVATE JOHN PARR
Killed 21st August 1914

The Legacy

The cemeteries and memorials along the Western Front are now the most recognizable and permanent legacy of The Great War. The Imperial War Graves Commission, formed by Royal Charter in May 1917, was the first organisation of any nation to be given the responsibility of caring for war dead, a task of unprecedented scale and complexity that began before the war was over and the outcome certain. The soldiers who fought were from many different ethnic cultures, all social classes, military ranks and religions, and reconciling what was achievable, together with the public interest and respect for the dead and their families, was a massive undertaking. The Prince of Wales understood this when he said that 'it would be most unseemly that a matter of this kind should become in any way the subject of public controversy…'

Thankfully, the Commissioners, led by Sir Fabian Ware, got it right, and by stating that 'those who have given their lives are members of one family' regardless of rank, race, or creed, deserving 'an equal tribute of gratitude and affection', they identified the key principle. Repatriation of all the dead was not feasible, but more importantly, selective repatriation would have been divisive and unfair. Soldiers were buried close to where they died, and there would be no privileges afforded by rank or status. Individual religions and faiths were to be respected and, as Sir Edwin Lutyens identified, it was equally important to acknowledge that some of those who died had 'no faith'.

The cemeteries and memorials of all nations are now part of the landscape, 'in perpetuity', and will continue to be a reminder of past sacrifice as well as hopefully a warning to future generations that, above, all, war is terrible.

PRIVATE GEORGE ELLISON
Killed 11th November 1918

BIBLIOGRAPHY

Barton, Peter with Banning, Jeremy. The Somme, The Unseen Panoramas. Constable, 2011

Bond, Brian. Survivors of a Kind, Memoirs of The Western Front. Continuum, 2008

Bond, Brian. The Unquiet Western Front, Britain's Role in Literature and History. Cambridge, 2003

Crane, David. Empires of the Dead: How One Man's Vision Led to the Creation of WWI's War Graves (Fabian Ware). William Collins, 2013

Doyle, Peter. Geology of the Western Front. The Geologists' Association, 1998

Falls, Cyril. The First World War. Longmans, 1960

Farrar-Hockley, Anthony. Death of an Army. Wordsworth Editions, 1998 (first published 1967)

Gilbert, Martin. The First World War. Weidenfeld and Nicolson, 1994

Griffiths, Paddy. The Great War on the Western Front: A Short History. Pen & Sword 2008

Hamilton, Andrew and Reed, Alan. Stolen Lives, Dene House Publishing 2014

Headlam, Cuthbert. History of the Guards Division in The Great War 1915-1918. John Murray, 1924

Holmes, Richard. Riding the Retreat, Mons to the Marne, 1914 Revisited. Jonathan Cape, 1995

Holmes, Richard. Western Front. BBC, 1999

Holt, Major & Mrs. Battlefield Guide to the Somme. Pen & Sword, 2007

Holt, Major & Mrs. Battlefield Guide to Western Front-South. Pen & Sword, 2011

Holt, Major & Mrs. Battlefield Guide to Ypres Salient & Passchendaele. Pen & Sword, 2008

Horne, Alistair. The Price of Glory, Verdun 1916. Penguin Books, 1994 (first published 1962)

Hughes, Colin. Mametz – Lloyd George's 'Welsh Army' at the Battle of the Somme. Gliddon Books, 1990

Keegan, John. The Face of Battle. Jonathan Cape, 1976

Kipling, Rudyard. The Irish Guards in the Great War, The Second Battalion. Spellmount, 1997 (first published 1923)

Liddell Hart, BH. History of The First World War. Cassell, 1970 (first published 1930)

Masefield, John. The Old Front Line. Pen & Sword, 2003 (first published 1917)

Middlebrook, Martin. The First Day of the Somme. Allen Lane, 1971

Roberts, Andrew. Elegy, The First Day of the Somme. Head of Zeus, 2015

Roynon, Gavin. Ed. Ypres Diary 1914-15: The Memoirs of Sir Morgan Crofton. History Press Limited, 2011

Sheffield, Gary. Forgotten Victory: The First World War – Myths and Realities. Headline, 2001

Stamp, Gavin. The Memorial to the Missing of the Somme. Profile, 2006

Terraine, John. Mons, The Retreat to Victory. BT Batsford, 1960

Toland, John. No Man's Land, The Story of 1918. Eyre Methuen, 1980

White-Spunner, Barney. Horse Guards. Macmillan, 2006

WEBSITES

www.westernfrontphotography.com,
www.ww1revisited.com,
www.pierreswesternfront.punt.nl
www.longlongtrail.co.uk

PHOTOGRAPHER'S NOTES

The photographs in this book are the result of James's many trips to the battlefields over the last five years, with the biggest but most pleasurable challenge being the editing from many hundreds of photographs taken. Although all seasons are covered, it is those photographs taken in the autumn and winter, when there is less leaf on the trees and an absence of crops, that reveal the starkness of the landscape more clearly. Many images were taken at either dawn or dusk when the light is low and atmospheric, as well as in all kinds of weather conditions. In many cases the worse the weather, the better the photograph. This was particularly true of the visit to Verdun when it rained continuously for three days. James's flight over the Somme in a microlight, as a non-aviator was both exhilarating and terrifying in equal proportions, but it did reveal the landscape from a fresh angle.

We hope the photographs will in their small way give greater understanding to the tragic events of a century ago.

Should you wish to visit any of the places in this book please go to our Battlefield Tours website:

WWW.SILENTLANDSCAPE.COM

ACKNOWLEDGEMENTS

The authors would like to acknowledge and thank the many people who have encouraged, helped, advised and inspired them on this project, either directly or indirectly. Specifically, we would like to thank: Nigel Adderley, who re-introduced us after many years, hence the book; Alan Reed, who gave historical advice; Andrew Hamilton, who read the text several times and gave us historical advice and suggestions, and also his photograph of George Ellison's grave at St. Symphorien Cemetery; and Maurice Bott. Last but not least, our thanks go to Alice Kerr and Charlotte Rowe for all their help and support. Some of our ideas about the landscape and regeneration derive from Charlotte's First World War garden. 'No Man's Land' at the Chelsea Flower Show, 2014. – James Kerr and Simon Doughty